When Raccoons Fall through Your Ceiling

The Handbook for Coexisting with Wildlife

Andrea Dawn Lopez

Foreword by Lynn Marie Cuny

Number Three in the Practical Guide Series

University of North Texas Press
Denton, Texas

Permissions:
University of North Texas Press
P.O. Box 311336
Denton, TX 76203-1336

The paper used in this book meets the minimum requirements of the American National Standard for Permanence of Paper for Printed Library Materials, z39.48.1984. Binding materials have been chosen for durability.

Library of Congress Cataloging-in-Publication Data

Lopez, Andrea Dawn, 1971–
When raccoons fall through your ceiling : the handbook for coexisting
with wildlife / Andrea Dawn Lopez.
p. cm. — (Practical guide series ; no. 3)
Includes bibliographical references (p.   ).
ISBN 1-57441-154-3 (cloth : alk. paper)
1. Urban pests—Control. 2. Wildlife pests—Control. 3. Animal
welfare. 4. Animal rescue. I. Title. II. Practical guide series
(Denton, Tex.) ; v. 3.
SB603.3 .L67 2002

2002007557

Be advised that there are many things to take into consideration when reading this book. The first is that wild animals are unpredictable and should, therefore, never be directly handled. Any involvement with a wild animal is at your own risk. Wild animals can cause severe injuries and even death. It is recommended that you consult a state wildlife agency or a rehabilitation center in any situation involving an encounter with a wild animal. In most states, it is illegal to handle or keep wild animals without the proper permits and you could face fines and jail time for breaking such laws.

Additionally, be advised that household products such as ammonia are only intended for uses as specified on the labeling. Federal law prohibits using a product in a manner other than the manner in which it was intended to be used. Wildlife rehabilitation centers across North America suggest using moth balls, naphthalene flakes, or household ammonia to aid in repelling animals. If you choose to use such products, be sure to exercise proper caution. Some people are physically sensitive to these products. The author, Andrea Dawn Lopez, and the University of North Texas, its officials, employees, and agents are not liable for any personal injuries or property damage resulting from your decision to handle wild animals or use any of the products suggested by rehabilitations centers.

Design by Angela Schmitt
Chapter title drawings by Sandy Ferguson Fuller

When Raccoons Fall through Your Ceiling: The Handbook for Coexisting with Wildlife is
Number Three in the Practical Guide Series

Dedication

To all the animals who have seen such suffering
because of things we have done.

To all those who have passed from this life because of that.

To those who now must live their lives behind wire enclosures,
never returning to a life they once knew.

To those who will never know the beauty of life they are missing.

To all those animals who have taught us so much
because of all that.

Contents

Foreword

O ver the past 25 years I have had innumerable opportunities to listen firsthand to the human perception of non-human animals. I have heard people express great concern for the well-being of baby raccoons, opossums, squirrels, and skunks. I have heard their expressions of awe and respect as they watched mother owls, foxes, and mockingbirds feed and care for their young. And I have listened as they rationalized the killing of snakes, bats, and mice. One common thread that seems to run through the hearts and minds of us humans is that we are, for better and worse, fascinated with wild animals. We put out feeders for birds, but are angry when squirrels feast at the feeders as well. We want to attract the "beautiful birds," but are offended when we see our feeders covered up with sparrows. We are outraged when raccoons curiously investigate our garbage cans and opossums take up residence under our houses. Day after day we seem to forget that every square inch we occupy was not so very long ago home to a diverse variety of wild animals. All too often what begins as fascination turns sourly into resentment and anger. It's time to take another look at the wild animals who share the urban and suburban spaces we all call home.

Ms. Lopez tackles a wide and extensive variety of common and not so common situations that occur when human and non-human worlds clash. In her book you will find creative and always humane ways to deal with the wild animals with whom you are neighbors. Even if you are simply looking for ways to discourage urban wildlife, you will be touched by the obvious respect for animals that is the basis for her book. If you are fortunate enough to live in a habitat that is enhanced by the presence of diurnal and nocturnal wild birds, reptiles, and mammals, then you will recognize and appreciate much of the information in these pages. Ms. Lopez always takes into consideration a view of the world from the non-human perspective while remembering that the goal of her book is to guide people gently into the ways of peaceful living with wildlife. She firmly balances the needs of both worlds, which, in fact, are really one world shared by many.

Lynn Cuny
Founder, Wildlife Rescue and Rehabilitation, Inc.

This permanent resident emu is one of many exotic species now living in a sanctuary. Although Australian, emus are commercially raised in the United States for their meat, skin, and feathers.

Introduction

Have you ever had raccoons fall through your ceiling? Discovered a nest of sparrows in your hanging flower basket? Or how about woken up one morning to discover deer have nibbled on your flower garden, reducing those blooming buds to stems? If so, you're not alone. The paths of humans and wildlife cross all the time, and there are organizations out there to make sure those paths cross as peacefully as possible!

Wildlife Rescue and Rehabilitation, Incorporated (WRR) is one of those. It was founded by Executive Director Lynn Cuny, in 1977 in San Antonio, Texas. The sanctuary was incorporated as a non-profit organization in 1978 with the intention of providing rescue, rehabilitation, and release of orphaned, injured, and displaced wildlife.

Before the organization was founded, the people in the San Antonio area had to rely on police and firefighters to solve their wildlife problems. There was no organization that had the proper training and expertise to handle the multitude of situations involving wild animals. Many wild animals were trapped and killed by people who thought that killing was the only way to solve the problem. Other people worked in vain to try and figure out ways to solve the conflicts on their own.

When volunteers and staff members with WRR first began working with the public, they encountered problems that included squirrels trapped in houses, raccoons living in attics, bats trapped in commercial buildings, as well as many other situations. During WRR's first year in operation, staff and volunteers rescued more than 60 wild animals. All of those rescues came after the public, police officers, and firefighters called the sanctuary for help.

After just three years, this non-profit organization was swamped with calls. That forced staff and volunteers to move what was a backyard operation to a four-acre site just outside the city limits of San Antonio. As the number of rescued animals increased, so did the donations from the public, helping to fund the growing sanctuary. The organization also began to acquire a solid membership base.

By 1985, WRR was caring for more than 1,200 animals each year. Many of these animals were orphaned, injured, and displaced. Others were victims of the exotic pet trade. For example, de-clawed bobcats and mountain lions came to the sanctuary. They were once prized pets and fads, but they also became big burdens to their owners. The organization took these animals in as permanent residents, giving them the environment to live out the rest of their lives. They could never be returned to their native environments because of their physical alterations and the fact that they were too comfortable around and dependent on humans.

People continued to bring wild animals to the sanctuary. The four-acre site was rapidly becoming inadequate. Then, in June 1985, a devastating flood nearly destroyed the sanctuary. Everyone was in desperate need of a new site and more money.

Through various fundraising activities and donations, WRR got the funding it needed for a new sanctuary within a year. That money helped to buy a 21-acre site about 10 miles outside of Boerne, Texas. Even that sanctuary became too small over time! In 2001, staff and volunteers began the tedious task of moving parts of the operation to a nearby site nearly 200 acres in size.

WRR is nationally recognized as an accredited wildlife rehabilitation sanctuary. It's a permanent home to more than 100 wild and exotic animals, and it serves as a temporary sanctuary to more than 5,000 wild animals each year.

The sanctuary is not open to the public. This is to give recuperating wildlife a chance to rest, heal, and live in an environment similar to what they'd have in the wild. WRR is adamantly against putting any animal on cement or in a sterile environment. Rather, animals are sheltered in spacious, secure enclosures filled with natural flora, large trees, and man-made shelters, providing them with privacy and security.

In the world outside of the sanctuary, staff and volunteers at WRR answer a 24-hour wildlife hotline, 365 days a year. Volunteers also travel to schools, civic organizations, and other places to help teach people about wildlife.

Between 10 and 15 paid staff members (depending on the season) work at the sanctuary, caring for sick, injured, and young animals. They also answer the thousands of phone calls that come in each year. About 200 volunteers assist the staff, working on fundraising, administrative tasks, animal rescues, and other projects in addition to animal care.

The sanctuary relies solely on donations from the private sector, from its membership of more than 7,000 individuals, and from funding from corporations, foundations, and private trusts. The generosity of the public is what funds the massive effort to care for all of the injured and orphaned animals each year.

There are many other sanctuaries across the United States and Canada with similar stories. What they all have in common is that they're working to help wild animals and educate the public about how to get along better with these creatures. This book is an effort to help them get their message out.

Many of the stories in *When Raccoons Fall through Your Ceiling* stem from my experience as a manager at WRR during 1994 and 1995. Much of the information and advice in the book is a combination of what its staff is trying to teach the public and what other wildlife specialists doing rehabilitation work across North America are saying. I've spent years researching this information, and I've tried to sift through it all and reiterate key points for the public. I chose these particular chapter subjects to write about because these seem to be the most common of all the wildlife-related problems—problems like finding baby wild animals, wildlife nesting in attics and chimneys, deer destroying gardens, amongst others.

There are some things you should take into consideration when reading this book. The first is that wild animals are unpredictable.

Most wild animals should never be directly handled. Any involvement you have with a wild animal is at your own risk. Wild animals, even the ones that look cute and cuddly, can cause severe injuries or even death. Consulting a state wildlife agency or a rehabilitation center is probably the best thing to do in each situation. In most states, it's illegal to handle or keep wild animals without the proper permits. You could face hearty fines and jail time for breaking that law. Exceptions are when you are working with rehabilitation centers to try and transport the animal to them.

Another thing to take into consideration is that household products like ammonia are only intended for uses specified on the labeling. Federal law prohibits using a product in any other way than that for which it was intended. Wildlife rehabilitation centers across North America suggest using moth balls, naphthalene flakes, or household ammonia to aid in repelling animals. Again, if you choose to do this, be cautious. Some people are physically sensitive to these products. If you are, you may want to try repelling wild animals with other things like lights, radios, one-way doors, etc., before trying anything else.

Lastly, the repelling techniques in this book have worked in many situations, but there's always the chance that for some reason or another, they may not work in your situation. Wild animals can become accustomed to things like motion-activated lights, bags of human hair, and commercial repellents over time. You may have to try several techniques to get the results you're looking for.

Some people say that ultrasonic pest repellents, for example, work. Others say they aren't effective and that the manufacturers' claims are false. Some of the commercial repelling devices are fairly new and have not yet developed a track record. If you're planning to buy commercial products, including sprays, liquids, or powders, check out their track record. They may work great, but they may not. Keep in mind that other options are available to repel wild animals.

Effective repelling is often effective after trial and error. It will take persistence, patience, common sense, and trying a combination of things before you find the methods that will work well for your situation. You may even invent your own techniques in the process!

You may notice that throughout this book, I refer to wild animals as "he" and "she." I do this to remind us all that animals do have gender, and that they aren't objects. At WRR, all the staff members were taught to refer to animals this way. That practice breeds a greater respect towards animals, recognizing them as individuals. I try to accomplish this in this book as well.

The purpose of this book is to make valuable information available to the public in written form. Wildlife rehabilitators across the world spend hour upon hour talking on the phone to people, teaching in classrooms, and going to people's houses to try and show them about how to better cohabit with wild animals. I wanted to put their efforts into a book that can serve as a manual for wildlife-related problems and concerns. It was written to try and help people with their struggles. I hope this guide will be available for your pleasure, or when you're having trouble reaching a wildlife rehabilitation center for advice.

All of the wildlife rehabilitation centers across the world exist because there is a need for education. The key to better living with wild animals is education. That will help our paths cross more peacefully in this world that we both share. Most every one of us will find a baby bird fallen from the nest, or have our flowers or crops in our gardens munched by deer. A better understanding of these situations will help ease resentment and promote more respect for wild animals.

Animals have always been a part of our environment, a part of our world. I believe they are also a part of our soul and that we need them to survive. If we don't learn to coexist with one another, modern civilization will eventually destroy all of the precious wildlife, and our souls will be empty because of it.

1

When Raccoons Fall through Your Ceiling

The sanctuary was a place where hundreds of species of animals and a handful of human caretakers lived in harmony, aside from the occasional incident where our two worlds overlapped in a far from graceful manner. I would have never guessed a weak ceiling in the old farm house would be to blame for one of those incidents.

The two-level wooden farm house was the heart of the sanctuary. It sat on 21 acres of Texas hill country with a little green pond out back. The entire place was enclosed by a 12-foot-high fence. A dirt road took you from the front gate, through thick cedar trees and brush, about a half mile to the house. It served as an office, nursery, critical care unit, and, at one time, employee sleeping quarters.

Driving down the dusty driveway was an adventure. It was like driving through a mini-safari. In the spring, white-tailed fawns frolicked in the fields to the left, while wild rabbits and javelinas foraged for food together in an enclosure to the right. If I looked closely through fencing that enclosed thick oak and cedar trees, I could see great horned owls perched on branches there, blending in with the landscape. White-winged doves pecked at seed in brown wooden cages along the way, recuperating before their release back into the wild.

Eventually that road widened into a massive dirt parking lot. Primate enclosures bordered the left side of it, holding caramel-colored Japanese macaques, crab-eating macaques, and lemurs. A gray brick food-preparation building called the nutrition center sat to the right. Staff would come and go with wheelbarrows of feed tubs filled with cat food, dog food, raw chicken, vegetables, and fruit—meals for many of the animals.

Straight ahead, a narrow sidewalk led the way to the house through two large, chicken-wire aviaries. They were full of all kinds of doves, herons, egrets, colorful parrots, even an exotic bird or two like a black Asian starling or myna bird. The myna bird was once someone's pet. Even though that was a part of his past and he was living in a spacious enclosure as just a bird, he still greeted every passerby with a "hello" in perfect English. His English, blended with the songs of all the birds, was a choir that could be quite deafening.

All these creatures helped to paint our picture of harmony. From the old, squinty-eyed gray tomcat who claimed his place on the front porch and the brown spiders crouched in their webs all around the screen door, to the families of raccoons that clumsily tromped through the attic of the house, the picture showed that all creatures could live together.

Black vultures are just one of many different species of animals that live at the Wildlife Rescue sanctuary. The birds pictured here aren't injured; they just hang out hoping for a free meal.

While it was a wonderful and often surprising experience to open a closet in my bedroom at the sanctuary and find a raccoon sitting there, or to wake up in the morning and find a flock of geese peering through my window at me, living amongst wild creatures wasn't always a pleasant experience.

The house that served as our rehabilitation center was aging, and sections of the ceiling were beginning to weaken. One day, as some of us worked in the office answering numerous phone calls from people with wildlife problems, we heard what sounded like a piece of heavy furniture being thrown down stairs.

We ran into the nursery area, which was now filled with puffs of dust and pieces of plaster. One of those weak sections of ceiling had finally given way to seven full-grown raccoons who must have weighed about 30 pounds each. Dazed, confused, and covered in pieces of ceiling, they scattered throughout the nursery, desperate to find a way out of this new and unfamiliar place they had fallen into.

A jagged gaping hole about three feet in diameter exposed one of the luckier raccoons who didn't fall through with the others. He remained perched on the edge, curiously watching all the excitement below.

We spent at least a half hour trying to herd all the raccoons toward open doors. Finally, we were successful and watched as the last one loped out the door and into the cover of some nearby oak trees.

At Wildlife Rescue and Rehabilitation, Inc., we followed our own advice. We did all that we could to live peacefully amongst wild animals. But the above example shows that there will be an occasion or two when your path will cross with that of a wild animal—or several wild animals—and that junction won't always be a smooth one.

You may have already crossed paths with a wild animal. Many home owners have. People living in suburban areas aren't the only ones who live there. Urban wildlife or wild animals have either chosen or been forced to live amongst us. They're all around our neighborhoods and homes.

These wild animals find their homes in the nooks and crannies of our homes and buildings, which provide safe havens for them. At any given time you could find a family of skunks living under your house, or a family of raccoons nesting in your chimney. Hanging plants are a popular choice for bird nests, and flower beds and gardens are often delicious buffets for deer.

For some people, the wild animals aren't bothersome. But for other people, living with wildlife is a difficult and sometimes scary experience. Fortunately, there are things that you can do to try and resolve your problems, solutions that will let you—and the wild animals— live in peace. After all, you both live here. If wild animals are to be preserved for the future you have to find a peaceful solution.

You may wonder how raccoons and skunks and foxes wound up living in your neighborhood in the first place. The truth is, they have been there all along. You see, your house is sitting on the ground that was once their home. Now, you both live in that place.

Urban sprawl has forced wild animals to make a choice. They can either follow the shrinking wilderness, or try to find new shelter in our neighborhoods. Many choose to stay in the territory they've always known. Besides, they find our chimneys, gardens, sheds, attics, and other little places around our homes quite suitable. They also like our homes because our garbage, gardens, and pet food offer them gourmet meals every day. People who feed their pets outside may not realize that they're inviting wild animals like skunks, raccoons, and foxes in for a snack.

Taking away these free meals is a good way to start discouraging wild animals from coming around. Almost every wild animal loves to eat cat and dog food. You may attract anything from magpies to skunks. Don't invite them back. Bring it all inside. Also bring in water dishes, especially at night. Animals that are nocturnal, like raccoons and skunks, will begin looking for "breakfast" as the sun starts to go down. These animals are also thirsty and will come in search of water.

You may think your pet's food and water are safe in your garage. But if you have a pet door in that garage, expect some uninvited guests for dinner. Wild animals are getting quite accustomed to our ways of life, and some aren't bashful when it comes to walking right into your home for a free meal.

If your dog or cat uses a pet door to get into the garage—or even your kitchen—you may want to invest in a door that is triggered by an electronic signal from your pet's collar. You could also try keeping the door locked at night when many wild animals are out and about.

It may be too late for all this prevention advice. You may have already discovered a raccoon or a skunk in your garage or a opossum in your kitchen, munching away on your food!

This is exactly what happened to a San Antonio man one night when he returned home from dinner. He said he walked into his kitchen, set his keys on the table, and then stopped short when he heard "crunching noises."

The man couldn't figure out where the noises were coming from. He sat and listened awhile before he realized the crunching was com-

11

ing from inside his pantry! He opened the door and found a opossum sitting inside a box of crackers "munching away."

The man had called our wildlife hotline for advice. We told him to put on gloves and just take the entire box of crackers—opossum and all—outside and let the little guy go away on his own. He followed our instructions and the opossum did go on his way, fat and happy after a free and easy dinner!

The fact that the opossum was already inside a cracker box made that man's situation easy to solve. Other situations may take a bit more work. If you ever come home and find a wild animal in your garage, the first thing to do is to open the garage door and turn on the light. The animal will head toward the darkest area, which at night will be outside.

If this doesn't happen right away, try turning on a radio. Turn up the volume to make it noisy. This will help encourage the animal to leave. You can also put household ammonia to work for you. Soak some old rags in it and toss them near the animal. The smell will help drive him away.

If you do use ammonia, respect the fact that this product wasn't made for repelling animals. It was made for household cleaning. The Food and Drug Administration does have labeling that specifically says this. If for some reason the product is irritating your skin or eyes, don't use it anymore!

As you're working to get the wild animal out of your garage, remember never to corner that animal or pick him up. Wild animals don't understand us, as we don't entirely understand them. They will become defensive when they feel threatened. Their only means of defense is to scratch and bite, especially against someone more than ten times their size! Gently encourage an animal to leave, giving him an obvious escape route. That's the best way for both of you to avoid confrontation. Most of the time the animal will be as eager to get away from you as you are for him to go.

When wild animals aren't trying to eat food inside your garage, they may be trying to eat food outside of your garage. By this I mean your trash. Remember, your trash could be a wild animal's treasure.

Many small mammals are omnivorous, meaning they will eat basically everything: fruits, vegetables, and meat scraps. Even coyotes are attracted to fruit like melons. You never know what species of wildlife will be rummaging through your trash bags and trash cans to find any goodies you've thrown away.

Wild animals are drawn to these leftovers in the trash by their sense of smell. Take some of that smell away by rinsing all of your cans and cartons with soapy water or a bleach solution before you put them out for recycling or throw them in the trash. If you leave your trash cans outside overnight, make sure they have lock down lids. You can also secure the lids with chains or bungee cords, but make sure that they are strong enough for even the most clever raccoon. If you live in a heavily wooded area or an area that has bears, purchase a steel bear-proof trash can. Usually your local state wildlife agency will have information on how to get one.

If you think you're alone in your struggles to find the best bungee cords and locking lids for your trash cans, you're not. People in suburbs across North America are struggling with the same wild animal conflicts, and it doesn't stop there. In fact, one of Colorado's most popular tourist attractions has struggled with the very same problem, and employees had to learn the hard way that it needed some very special trash cans.

The Royal Gorge draws in more than 500,000 visitors each year. They come to see the highest suspension bridge in the United States, spanning 1,053 feet over the Arkansas River below.

The visitors at the Royal Gorge have quite a hike when they come visit. The bridge is long and some of the best vantage points are at the tops of rocky, steep hills that'll have you huffing and puffing in no time. Hence, there's plenty of food and drink at the park as well, anything from hamburgers and hot dogs, to funnel cakes and ice cream.

Some of those visitors, however, didn't come to see the magnificent bridge, but rather all that greasy food. Those visitors tended to get a little rowdy and destructive when they didn't get what they wanted. Those visitors were black bears, frequenting the park for half-eaten burgers and hot dogs in the trash cans, greasy grills, and even fresh food stored in coolers.

It didn't take employees long to figure out that they had a problem. The bears tipped over, tossed around, and destroyed nearly 20 trash cans, pushed over fences, and knocked down outdoor coolers. It was just part of their routine for getting dinner each night. After replacing all those trash cans at a few hundred dollars a piece, the bridge company's employees realized they had to do something to fix the problem. They contacted the Division of Wildlife for help.

After some consultation, the employees were on a mission, a mission to get one message to the bears: they were going to have to find their evening snacks elsewhere!

Employees started picking up all the trash at the end of the day after all the food vendors closed. They put up an eight-foot chain-link fence around its trash storage site—a fence with concrete reinforcement on the bottom and barbed wire across the top. They bolted all the coolers down, as well as the grease traps from the cooks' kitchens, and they started spraying down their walk-in freezers with bleach to get rid of any food smells.

The final step was installing several bear-proof trash cans in the picnic areas. The cans are configured for humans only. You have to slip your hand underneath a lip to release a lever to open the lids. It's a space that's too small for a big bear paw. If those spaces weren't that small, the bears may actually be able to figure out how to open those trash cans!

The entire project took many hours of hard work, but it was successful. Some officers from the Colorado Division of Wildlife like to point out this incident as one that homeowners can learn from. It offers good guidelines that they can follow for their own homes.

The Division took that example a step farther in September 2001, stating that homeowners and businesses that continually leave trash and other attractants within reach of bears will be fined. This was an emergency regulation that the Colorado Wildlife Commission approved at the request of wildlife officers. Officers said that people were continually ignoring their requests to keep trash, food, bird seed, and pet food out of reach of bears. The tickets are mainly for repeat violators, as well as people who purposely put food outside so they can watch the bears come around and eat. The Division is also trying to encourage local cities and counties to adopt ordinances that require bear-proof trash cans. These are a good way to help end this conflict.

Bears might be a problem at your house, and you may be surprised to know that it might not be trash and pet food that are drawing them in, but rather, bird food.

If you're a bird lover in bear territory, chances are you're inviting bears in as well. Sound crazy? Bears absolutely love bird seed and hummingbird food. Just ask anyone at the Bear Creek Nature Center in Colorado Springs, Colorado.

The center wasn't named after all the bears in the area, but the name took on an entirely new meaning once some area bears figured out that it was a perfect place for some of their favorite delicacies.

These bears weren't shy. In fact, they'd come strolling down the sidewalk in the middle of the day and walk right up to any one of the many bird feeders at the nature center. The bird feeders sat on metal poles. The bears bent all of those poles, toppling the feeders over before they began cleaning up all the seed like vacuum cleaners. They also tackled the hummingbird feeders to get at the sweet sugary liquid inside.

Of course, the bears didn't stop there. They also knocked over all the trash cans, scattering trash throughout the parking lot. For awhile, the bears became as much of an attraction as the nice hiking trails and assortment of wild birds.

One group of hikers was absolutely startled one day as they walked around their parked car to the sidewalk. They stopped dead in their tracks when they saw a big black bear lying on the sidewalk between them and their favorite hiking trail. The bear was sunning himself and drying off after taking a stroll through the stream at the bottom of the hill. Eventually he got up and walked away, leaving a big, wet, bear butt print on the sidewalk.

The bears never hurt anyone. In fact, they were glad to go on their way and avoid a confrontation with humans whenever they could.

The nature center personnel, however, had to completely change the way they did things. Volunteers now bring in all of the humming-bird and bird feeders at night. They store their bird food in metal trash containers with locking lids. They've also built new trash cans that are enclosed in wooden boxes with locking lids—trash cans that can't be tipped over.

It sounds like a great deal of work, and it is, but nature center staff and volunteers are glad to do it. One volunteer told me that if we want to live in this beautiful country, we have to live with the ani-mals that also make it their home. She said if you get rid of all the animals, taking them out of the habitat, it destroys the entire habi-tat. She said what affects and destroys the habitat will eventually affect and destroy us too. It will come full circle. In order to better live with these animals, however, many of us need to learn more about their behavior and how to cohabit.

When I was about ten years old, I remember waking up in the middle of the night to loud footsteps on our roof. Our house had been bur-glarized years before, and I was sure that it was happening again, only this time while we were sleeping, rather than out of the house for the evening.

Paralyzed with fear, I managed to slip out of my bed and tip toe down the hallway to my parents' bedroom where I woke up my mom and dad. I told them that I was hearing noises on the roof above my bedroom and out on the patio outside my window.

Concerned, my parents quietly tip toed back to my bedroom with me and we opened my blinds and looked outside. The moon was full, giving us quite a bit of light to see everything that was in the yard. Then, we heard the loud footsteps again, only this time they were getting closer to the edge of the roof where it met the patio cover in the backyard. We kept watching.

After only about a minute, we saw the "burglars." Those burglars were common raccoons. We saw a giant mother, probably weighing around 40 pounds, and her five babies. They were doing their best to stay in a single-file line behind her. Since raccoons are nocturnal, meaning they're most active at night, they were wide awake, full of energy, and even playful as they made their way through their moon-lit territory in search of food. Of course, my parents and I could only sigh in relief. Living with wild animals takes some getting used to.

There are several things you can do to keep raccoons and other wildlife from using your house as their stomping grounds.

One great way to keep animals off of your home is to make it inaccessible to them. Prune any nearby trees back at least 10 to 15 feet from the roof so that even the best jumper can't gain access. Remove all of the lower branches on your trees and encircle the trunks in metal cylinders or cones that are at least three feet high. This will keep animals from climbing them, again, limiting any access they might have to the roof. If you're in the process of landscaping your house, plant trees at least 15 feet from the house.

It's a good idea to keep animals off your roof so you don't have to hear them running around up there, but keeping them off the roof will also keep them from building nests in your chimney. Raccoons, squirrels, and birds are some animals that commonly take up residence in chimneys. Cap your chimney to keep them from doing this, and keep your damper closed when you're not using the fireplace just in case any animals do take up residence there. This way, you won't have them trapped in your fireplace or even running around in your house.

This problem is more common than you might think. I once went over to an elderly woman's house in San Antonio to help her get a bird out of her fireplace. He had flown through the opening in her chimney, fallen down, and was unable to fly out once he reached the fireplace.

I could see he was a little sparrow before I even opened the glass doors. He was dirty, covered in soot, and tired from trying to fly out. I scooped him up and put him in a cardboard box. As I was doing that, I noticed six other dead sparrows lying in the soot. This woman had a chronic problem with birds becoming trapped in her fireplace. Unfortunately, the woman didn't notice this problem in time to save those other little birds. Fortunately for this little sparrow, she did. Capping your chimney is a good way to ensure that no matter how busy you are or how little attention you pay to your fireplace, you won't ever have this problem.

The chimney isn't the only place animals like to nest, however. Loose shingles and boards can make it easy for animals to gain access to your attic. Check the entire perimeter of your house for weak spots and secure them or seal them off. Make this a regular routine. Check the roof and eaves, and seal off any holes with materials like galvanized sheet metal, for example. Seal off any vents with rust-proof screens.

You may want to try putting an owl decoy on the roof or chimney to help out. Owls are a major predator of small mammals. The decoy could help to scare them away. You may have to move the decoy from time to time so that the animals don't become too used to it.

Motion-activated devices may also come in handy for you. These include motion-activated lights and ultrasonic pest repellents.

Motion-activated lights can be effective for scaring away nocturnal wildlife. These animals are accustomed to and most comfortable in the dark and don't appreciate bright light. Lights left on all night can help prevent animals from approaching your house. Many will tend to shy away from houses that are well lit. Motion-activated lights are good because they can be startling, and an animal would be less likely to get used to a light that wasn't always on. Use a minimum of 100 watts for every 15 square yards of yard space.

Ultrasonic pest repellents are devices that emit high-frequency noises that only animals can hear and that are generally irritating to their ears. These devices emit the tones when they detect motion. The irritating noise will usually cause animals to avoid the place where the sound is coming from.

These devices can be used indoors or outdoors, during the day or night. If you have a pet that stays in the yard, you may want to position the detectors so that they aren't activated by the pet's movement. The high frequency noise will be extremely irritating to your pet, and even more irritating if there's no escape from it!

When you're finished wildlife-proofing your home, the next step is to create a type of buffer around it, making the yard itself an unpleasant place for wildlife. You can do this by taking away any shelter that a wild animal might find comforting.

Clear all wood, brush, and rock piles. Wildlife like to hide in those. Try to store any wood off the ground in storage boxes. A six-foot fence can also help to keep some animals out of your yard.

You may already have a problem with an animal taking up or trying to take up residence in one of the nooks or crannies around your home. This calls for some trouble shooting. If you notice that an animal has been attempting to dig his way under your house, bury a layer of hardware cloth in the dirt.

Hardware cloth is similar to chicken wire and you can get it at any local hardware store. You can use it to keep an animal from digging any farther in an isolated situation, but it's also a good idea to skirt the foundation of your home to prevent future digging. Cover up any holes with hardware cloth as well. This works best when you seal the hole and extend the wire a couple of feet into the ground, or outwards from the foundation in an "L" pattern.

If you're having a great deal of trouble in a particular area, sprinkle cayenne pepper around the area, and try partially burying jars of ammonia in the ground. You can refill them when they evaporate. The smell of the ammonia and the pepper are very irritating and will help discourage animals from digging any more. Remember to reapply the pepper after it rains!

If you already have an animal living under your porch, shed, or home and you want to get that animal out, you'll have to make his home an unpleasant place to be. Wild animals generally like dark, quiet areas. Your job is to change all that.

It's best to wait until an animal is out and about before you try to repel him. For nocturnal animals, this would be after dark. For diurnal animals, or animals that are most active during the day like squirrels, this would be during the day. You want the animals to be alert and awake so that they're able to search for a new home. If you repel them while they're sleeping, they'll be disoriented as they're chased from their home, and this could cause them a great deal of stress. An animal could wander into another one's territory and get into a fight. He could also wander onto a roadway and endanger himself in traffic.

You can either watch for the animal to leave his home, or sprinkle baby powder or flour on the ground and periodically check for tracks. This way, you know the animal is out and about.

Now's the time to try and make the animal's home unpleasant. You can soak several old rags in ammonia and toss them back into the animal's home. Tie knots in the middle of the rags so they're easier to throw, and toss them as far back as they'll go. Ammonia is useful because it has such a strong odor, but it also evaporates quickly so you don't have to smell it for very long.

Complement this repelling by sprinkling cayenne pepper into the area, blast a radio near or against the animal's home, and try to shine a light into the darkness, or turn on a strobe light in the area. You can also spread naphthalene flakes around. Naphthalene is the active ingredient in moth balls and it also makes the place smell unpleasant to the animal. Another suggestion is to use an ultrasonic device that will emit high-frequency, irritating sound waves that the animal won't like.

This combination of ammonia, naphthalene flakes, pepper, light, and noise should quickly cause the animal to leave. You may have to do this for several days in a row. Persistence is the key.

Patience is also a necessity, especially if that animal has babies. If you've accidentally tried to repel an animal with babies, you may not have to worry too much. The parent or parents will generally pick up the babies and move them to a new location. What you should do, however, is wait to seal the entrance until the babies have grown up and left the nest, so to speak. This would take an immense amount of pressure off the parent. After all, think about what it would be like trying to care for young and finding a new home all at the same time!

Trying to repel an entire family could also cause the young to be abandoned. In that case, you'll be stuck with the babies and if you don't care for them and get them to a wildlife rehabilitator, they'll die in that cranny under your home, porch, or shed. Then you'll have to find a way to remove the dead animals or deal with the stench. If you can wait, try not to repel or seal up the entrance until either late winter before an animal has babies, or until it starts to get substantially colder in the fall. You can also monitor the family. When the babies are nearly full grown and following their mother out of the den or nest, that's a better time to try and repel the family.

If you're trying to repel more than one animal and you're having trouble monitoring all of them, you can try setting up a one-way door that allows the animal to exit, but not to get back in. You can also try the above-mentioned repelling methods.

After repelling for several days, you're going to want to be sure that the animal has indeed found another home. There are a few ways to make sure that has happened. The first is to sprinkle flour or baby powder around the entrance to the animal's home. If you don't see tracks, the animal most likely has left. If you do see tracks, you know you'll have to keep repelling for a few more days.

Another way to check and see if an animal is coming or going is to set up a piece of cardboard in the entrance to the home. If the cardboard is pushed aside, again, you'll know the animal probably hasn't found a new home.

Give the animal a few days to relocate. When you're sure he's gone, that's the time to board up the crevice so that no other animal takes up residence there again. Extend the board at least six inches beyond the edges of the opening to safeguard against gnawing. Once the entrance is sealed up, be sure to monitor that area for a few days. If an animal is trapped inside, he'll probably be gnawing or scratching, trying to get out. In that case, you'll have to pry off that board and let him out.

Throughout my childhood, it seemed we had a different family living with us each year—a different family of wild animals, that is. My parents' house has a long, one-foot-wide passageway that runs under the back of the house, parallel to the patio. One end of it had always been wide open, inviting whomever to come and live there.

One year, we had a wild black cat that lived under our house. Another year we had a wild rabbit that lived there. Every other year for about five years, we had a family of skunks that lived under our house. My dad finally boarded up that entrance one year and that ended the live-in program at the Lopez residence!

It might be that you don't have an animal living under your home, but rather above your home in the attic. Squirrels, raccoons, and small rodents seem to love making homes out of attics, and it's a very common problem.

You can follow all of the above procedures to repel animals from your attic. Even though you may not know where the animals are getting in, remember that when there's a way in, there's also a way out. The repelling techniques should drive the animal right back out the way he came in. Once you've found the hole and you're sure the animal is gone, board it up.

People who have animals living in their attic commonly have a related problem with those animals falling down into walls and becoming trapped. These situations usually involve baby animals. Lost and confused without mom, the baby is disoriented and unable to crawl back out on his own.

The best thing to do is dangle a sheet or a knotted rope down into the wall. You can find most openings to walls in the attic. Secure the sheet or rope at the top so that the animal is able to crawl out. Then, leave the area. Squirrels and raccoons are excellent climbers and should easily find their way out in a short amount of time. Sometimes, a young animal may be too young to climb. He may not have the strength or the coordination to use that rope or knotted sheet. Call a wildlife rehabilitation center for advice. The only way to get that animal out may be by cutting a hole in the wall.

Whatever you do, try to act quickly in a situation like this. If you don't, the animal could die. Not only would that be unfortunate, but if that animal dies, he will rot and leave a stench in your wall. A professional may charge hundreds of dollars to come to your house, open up the wall, and remove that animal.

There's one more common situation where you may have to use the above repelling techniques, and that's when you have animals nesting in your chimney. Don't try to smoke the animals out. Use the bright light, radio, and ammonia in your fireplace to drive the animals out.

A related problem in this situation is baby animals falling from the chimney into the fireplace. You can rescue the baby the same way you'd rescue one that has fallen into a wall, by dropping a knotted rope or sheet through the opening in the top and letting it dangle all the way to the bottom into the fireplace. The baby may use the rope or sheet to climb out.

If he doesn't, you can remove the baby another way. Put on a pair of leather gloves. Then, gently throw a pillowcase or towel over the animal to cover him up and calm him down. Then, lay a cardboard box on its side and, using something like a broom, push the animal into the box. Make sure there's bedding on the bottom of the box,

If you have a baby squirrel who's been separated from his mother, put him in a box with bedding and put him outside. Hopefully, the two will be reunited.

secure it, and take it outside. Place it near the chimney. Make sure all pets are out of the area, open up the box, and leave. The parent should come around and take the baby back.

If this is a nocturnal animal like a raccoon, you want to do this at night when the parent is out and about. If it's a diurnal animal like a squirrel or a bird, you want to do this in the day when the parent will be around to see the baby. You can even place the box on the roof beside the chimney or in a tree near the chimney.

If you don't have an animal stuck in your house, you may have one stuck in your yard. One last common encounter you might have is finding an animal like a raccoon or a opossum sitting in a tree. This is nothing unusual. Sometimes wild animals do hang out in trees during the day. Often they're just resting there until they venture out at dark. They should be gone by then.

An animal might not leave if you have a dog, however. Dogs often frighten animals into staying in trees throughout the evening. If you want the animal to leave, put your dog inside the house or garage. This will give the animal a chance to calm down and leave the area. As long as the animal is frightened and can hear the dog barking, he won't leave. This is the animal's way of protecting his life! Even if you have a dog that wouldn't hurt a fly, that wild animal has no way of knowing that. He'll stay in the tree until what he perceives as the danger is gone.

This chapter may have given you several solutions that you think are too time-consuming. You might wonder why it's better to try these techniques rather than try something like live-trapping and relocating. The answer is that the above-mentioned techniques address the source of the problem. Live-trapping is merely a band-aid solution.

Live-trapping doesn't solve anything. The reason is because most animals are territorial, so once an animal has been trapped and relocated to another place, another animal will recognize that the space is available and move in.

Live-trapping and relocating are also dangerous for wildlife. Taking an animal to a new place can stress the wildlife already there, as well as the animal you just relocated. Some wildlife rehabilitators say the mortality rate among relocated animals is extremely high because they're unable to find food and shelter in a brand new area. They're also intruding on other wildlife's territory, which can result in fights and competition for food.

Another downside to relocating is that you could be transferring a sick animal. That animal could then spread sickness to healthy animals who may have otherwise not contracted the disease. A disease can die off in the area it's in. However, if you give it the chance to jump from one area to another, it generally will.

Finally, many animals are hit by cars while wandering. They may also have a hard time finding food in a wooded, natural area after having lived in an urban environment where food has been plentiful for so long.

Another similar, band-aid solution is setting out poison bait. Again, once one animal is gone, another will move in. Poison is extremely dangerous to other animals, as well, like housepets and other wild animals you might not mind having around. It's very likely that the wrong animal will eat the poison, or that the dead animal that ate the poison will be eaten by another animal, like a hawk, your dog, or your cat. That animal will then become poisoned and may die. If you poison an animal, it's also very likely that the animal could crawl under your home to die, leaving a smelly carcass.

You will never be completely rid of animals if you trap and relocate, or use poison. It will also cost you money to hire an animal exterminator, and again, it won't be solving the problem. Part of the problem is often that we, as humans, see living with wildlife as a problem. Just as trees, butterflies, and weeds are part of our environment, so are these animals.

Concentrate on making your home as unpleasant as possible and you will find that wild animals won't want to come around. If you don't want to do this yourself, you may be in luck. There are some people who make their living from wildlife-proofing homes. Perhaps one of those people lives in your area.

Trying the above procedures will save you money, time, unnecessary hassle, and will allow both yourself and indigenous wildlife to coexist.

Here is a summary of the advice in this chapter:

- bring in pet food and water at night
- secure pet doors at night
- secure trash and compost piles
- bring in hummingbird and bird feeders at night
- cover fish ponds
- prune back trees 10 to 15 feet from roof
- remove lower branches on trees
- encircle trunks in metal cylinders or cones
- plant new trees 15 feet from your house
- cap chimney
- put screens over vents
- secure loose shingles
- fix holes in roof or eaves
- fix holes or loose siding on house
- put owl decoy on roof
- install outdoor, motion-activated lights
- bury hardware cloth around foundation of home
- sprinkle cayenne pepper around
- clear all brush, rock, or trash piles

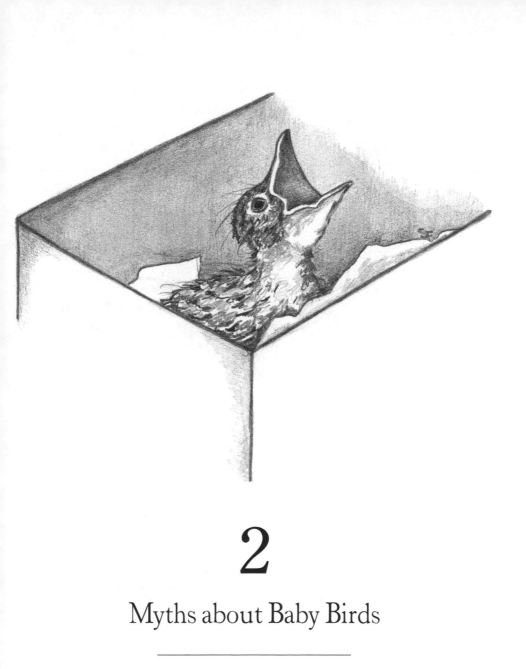

2

Myths about Baby Birds

───────────

The bird stood on the patio, wings limp and hanging at her sides. She stared into the window of the house—it seemed, right at the woman who watched from inside. The bird wouldn't move.

"I think she's depressed," the woman told me over the phone. "Is that possible, for a bird to be depressed? She's been standing there for almost an hour and she hasn't moved!"

The bird's baby had just died. The woman called the wildlife hotline to see what she should do.

The death came about after a long series of mistakes on this woman's part. The mother bird had built a nest right above the woman's doorway, but she was afraid all the commotion would be too dangerous for the mother and her baby. She was afraid that opening and shutting the door could cause the nest to fall.

In an effort to make sure the baby bird wouldn't be injured, she took the nest and baby inside her home and called the wildlife hotline. She didn't know what to do and she needed advice.

The first problem was, however, that she waited about two hours before calling the hotline. Parent birds feed their babies as often as every 15 minutes from dusk until dawn. After two hours, the little bird was becoming weak from no food.

The woman was told to put the nest and the bird back outside immediately so that the parent bird could continue to care for the baby. She was told that her human scent wouldn't cause the bird to abandon the little one. That's a common myth.

The woman put the nest back outside in a nearby tree and waited. But the second problem was that she was impatient. She didn't see the parent come around right away so she brought the nest back inside for awhile. Then, she tried putting the nest back outside, only this time she put it out on the back porch.

This woman had good intentions, but she wasted too much time. She was so concerned about where to put the nest that she didn't give the parent enough time to come back. In the meantime, the baby was getting weaker and weaker. He finally died.

It seemed the situation had come to an end, but it hadn't. That's when the woman called back, wanting to know if it was possible for this parent bird to be depressed. The woman tried to go outside and shoo the bird away, but she said the bird wouldn't leave.

The woman had guests coming over for a barbecue. She finally had to use a broom to gently push the bird into a nearby bush where she would be out of sight, and out of harm's way. Eventually the bird flew away, but not before she had taken this woman on a serious guilt trip and raised an interesting question of whether or not birds can be depressed.

We may not ever be able to answer that question, but we can do our best to prevent situations like the one above from ever happening again.

Baby bird calls are perhaps one of the most common types of phone calls wildlife sanctuaries have to deal with. At Wildlife Rescue, we would get a call from someone who had found a baby bird about every minute of the day during San Antonio's spring and summer months. This went on from about April until August, with an occasional baby bird call in March or September.

Baby birds can hatch consistently throughout the warmer months of the year, especially in climates that are moderately warm year-round. Some parent birds can hatch more than one nest full of babies during that time. But generally, you'll see the bulk of the baby birds in the spring.

Baby birds pop out of nests like popcorn. After they're born, it's very likely that they'll fall from the nest and spend some time on the ground. That's about the time that people find them, and most often, they'll take them home in an effort to save them and even raise them. You can't blame anyone. After all, these little birds look so frail and helpless, it seems like the best thing to do. But the reality is, a baby bird's best chance of survival is in the wild without you by his side.

Let's say you were able to take on the task of raising a baby bird, and do it successfully. By the time that bird is a teenager, he will identify you as his parent, making it nearly impossible for him to return to the wild and associate with other birds like himself. He'll have trouble finding food because he doesn't know how, and he could endanger himself by approaching another human. The process of becoming attached to a human is called imprinting. The bird becomes dependent on you and identifies humans as family.

We would often have people bring baby birds to us at the sanctuary that were in this exact situation. These people had found these birds as babies and cared for them until they were teenagers, full of feathers and ready to fly. About that time, their human caretakers generally came to their senses, realizing that they couldn't properly care for these birds any longer, and ethically realizing that the best place for them was in the wild. They'd bring these little teenage birds to the sanctuary and turn them over to us, hoping that we could teach them to be wild birds once again.

The process of teaching these little birds to act like others in their same species was difficult. First of all, we'd have to try to teach them to eat on their own by taking long forceps and dropping worms and other types of food in front of them until they learned how to pick up the food on their own.

We'd try to hide and stay out of sight so they wouldn't see much of humans anymore, but these little birds would fly out of their cages, perch on our shoulders, and scream in our ears to be fed. In fact, it seemed they were more comfortable perching on human shoulders than on tree branches where they should have been!

Eventually, after housing these little guys with other birds like themselves that weren't quite so friendly with humans, they'd begin to act more like birds—perching on branches, socializing with others, and foraging for food as they should. We'd use birds of the same species that weren't imprinted to teach the imprinted ones how to act like wild birds. Even so, it wasn't uncommon for one of these birds to relapse before the entire process was over.

When the teenage birds were ready to make the transition from their cages inside the nursery to outdoor flight cages, we'd transfer them and allow them to stay outside for a period of time to get accustomed to the weather. In those cages, they'd build up their flight muscles before they were finally released back into the wild.

I'd been carefully monitoring a group of blue jays until they had proved that they were ready to go. They were eating on their own, drinking on their own, their flight muscles were well developed, and they had a normal fear of humans—something all wild animals must have for their own protection.

I opened the door and watched the beautiful blue birds fly to their new lives one by one. Seeing them take off into the hill country and experience a real tree and the open sky for the very first time was entrancing. It's those precious moments a wildlife rehabilitator lives for, moments that are to be cherished and milked for all they're worth until they gently slip away.

I smiled and took a deep breath as that moment slowly slipped away, turning to walk back down the path toward the old farm house. After only a few steps, I heard the familiar sound of a blue jay begging for food. I stopped and turned around, but saw nothing. I kept walking, only to hear that familiar sound again. This time, when I turned around, I saw one of the young blue jays I had just released following me down the path. As I took a few steps forward, he'd follow, fluttering from tree to tree behind me.

This is something you don't want to see as a rehabilitator, a bird still looking toward humans for food after being released back into the wild. If that bird approached someone who didn't like birds or someone with a mean streak, he could wind up dead. This is the danger of imprinting young birds.

The good news with this little one, however, was that he had enough wild instinct in him to know what was best for him. Even though he fluttered from tree to tree behind me for awhile, when I'd try to approach him, he'd shy back like a wild bird and fly a short distance away. He hung around the outdoor aviaries with the other birds long enough for us to keep a close eye on him. He was able to fend for himself, and would never let us get too close. Eventually, he followed his call of the wild and left the sanctuary.

The sooner you can get an abandoned baby bird to a wildlife rehabilitator, the better. The bird probably won't become imprinted in that case, and it'll be easier to raise him and set him free without complications. However, if you can avoid taking a baby bird out of the wild altogether, that might be the best solution of all.

If you find a baby bird fallen from the nest or fluttering around near his home tree, usually the best thing to do is to put him back in the nest or leave him alone. The parent birds are most likely nearby, watching and waiting for you to leave so they can continue to care for their baby.

Even if you were to find a nest full of babies beside a tree that was just cut down, the best thing to do might be to secure their nest, babies and all, in another nearby tree. If you don't have a tree in your yard, try a neighbor's tree. You can even use your roof or a swingset, so long as the nest is up high. If you chose to use one of the latter options, be sure to provide shade for the baby birds so they're not baking in the sun. You can even get creative with making another nest. A small cat house with a roof and a hole for the opening may make the perfect nest, especially for species like owls. They may use a hollow in a tree for a nest and the cat house is similar to that. Putting the birds out again will give the parents a chance to care for them. They're probably lurking somewhere nearby, waiting for you to leave.

Before we talk more about what's best for baby birds, it's important that you understand how they develop. This will help you make

If you can't return a baby bird to his nest, put him in a box with bedding, as we did with this fledgling pigeon, and put that in the tree.

the best decision for a baby bird should you come across one some-day.

Baby birds basically develop in three stages. When most first hatch from their eggs, they're bald, pink, and their eyes are closed. This is the hatchling stage.

After this, they enter the baby or nestling stage where they begin to grow small pin feathers, or feathers that begin to emerge encased in a protective sheath. A baby in this stage will also begin to grow soft down.

Finally, the bird will enter the fledgling or teenager stage. The bird will grow all of his feathers and begin to flap his wings to build up wing muscles. This is the stage when the parent bird will teach the little one how to eat on his own, all the while continuing to feed and care for him.

If you happen to find a little pink bird or one with pin feathers, locate the nest and put the bird back. If you can't locate the nest, put the baby bird in a small cardboard box with some tissue on the bottom for bedding and secure it in the closest tree. The tissue will provide warmth and a stable, non-slip surface to grip onto. Don't use anything with holes or strings that may entangle the little bird's legs, and don't use a wire or mesh container. If you can see the nest but it's too high to reach, secure the cardboard box in the same tree but on a lower branch. Be sure not to put the little bird in full sun; he could get too hot and dehydrated.

The parent bird may take a few hours to get used to this new nest and location, but will eventually continue to care for the young again. Try not to waste any time, however, as you create this makeshift nest and secure it. It's not OK to say you'll do it right after an errand or lunch because the baby bird may starve to death in a matter of a few hours. Baby birds are fed often by their parents, and they me-tabolize their food at such a fast rate that if they go without eating for more than a half day, they can die.

It's also important to get the baby bird situated before the sun goes down. Most species of birds are active during the day only, and putting the babies back in a tree after sunset won't do them much good. You want to try to secure them and have the parents resume care before night falls. If you wait until after dark, the parents won't find the babies again until the morning and this may be too late for them.

There are exceptions to this rule, however. Some species of birds like owls and nighthawks are most active at night, going off in search of food only when the sun goes down. If you find a baby owl has fallen from the nest, try to reposition him at night when the parent is most active and can resume care. Occasionally an owl will resume care during the day. If you're unsure, call a wildlife rehabilitator for help.

The above-mentioned suggestions are for hatchlings or nestlings, but the rules for fledglings are a little bit different. Remember, fledglings are like teenagers—they have all their feathers and they're learning how to eat and fly on their own before they leave the nest for good. In preparation for this, they'll hop out of the nest and spend some time on the ground, learning how to pick up seeds or insects from the parent birds.

Since these birds can't quite fly yet, and because they're hopping around on the ground, they're often mistaken for birds that are injured and unable to fly. Fledglings will spend two to five days on the ground, all the while being supervised by the parent birds. During this time, a bird's feathers will grow and his wing muscles will develop as he tries to flutter around. Soon after that, he will be able to fly and follow his parents around from tree to tree until he ventures off on his own.

A fledgling is more vulnerable when he's on the ground. At night, a parent bird will often hide the little one in the bushes to protect him from predators. But a parent bird can't always protect a fledgling. Sometimes, the little bird will wind up in a high-traffic area like a sidewalk or a street.

If you find a fledging in this situation, it's OK to pick him up and move him to the safe cover of bushes or trees, or put him back in the nest if you can find it. Once the bird is safe, leave the area. Too much interaction with a wild bird can cause him a great deal of stress. He doesn't know you're trying to help him; he only knows you're not one of his own kind—you're probably a predator in his mind!

In some situations, you may have trouble finding trees or a nest to put the fledgling in. This may be because you've discovered a species of bird that nests on the ground. Species like this raise young in open fields, sometimes even in parking lots! Killdeer, in particular, are one species of bird that seem to love to pick asphalt fields as homes, and it's very likely you'll see their little ones running all over the place!

Try to identify the species in a bird book to help you confirm that this is a type of bird that nests on the ground. Meadowlarks and nighthawks are two other species that like to do this. If this is the case, try to move the babies to the cover of some brush if they're in a busy area. That's generally what the parents will do. They leave their young hidden in tall grasses and brush while they go out to search for food.

In any case, if you want to make sure the fledgling is doing OK, watch from a distance. You should see the fledgling interacting with a parent bird and sometimes following a parent from limb to limb on a tree. Watching from a distance is better for the birds, and yourself. If you get too close, the parent birds may squawk and dive-bomb you in an effort to protect their young. Some birds feign injury to turn your attention to them and lure you away from their young.

In any instance where you've relocated a baby bird, give the parents plenty of time to resume care for their baby—even as much as three hours. It's important to watch as closely as you can during that time because if you don't, you could miss a quick visit by a parent bird. It only takes a second for mom or dad to slip into the nest, feed the babies, and leave again. They could do this in the same time it would take you to get a glass of water or answer the phone.

It's also critical that you don't disturb the reunion by running outside to check on the babies every five minutes or so. If the parents are continually frightened, they may never come back. The more time it takes for the parent to return to the nesting area, the greater the chance that the baby bird is weakening from not being fed.

Stay out of sight and try to keep all pets out of the area. Dogs or cats can also frighten the parents and cause them to avoid the nest altogether. Remember, a fledgling will only be on the ground for a few days. If you can keep your cat or dog out of the area for that short amount of time, you'll help ensure the little bird will mature and fly off on his own. Cat attacks, in particular, are one of the major reasons baby birds never make it to adulthood.

Believe it or not, dog attacks aren't so far behind. Quite often, we would get calls from dog owners saying that a parent bird had built a nest in a tree in their dog's pen. Sometimes, when the baby birds would fall to the ground, the dogs would eat them. This is a dangerous situation for a family of birds and there is a way that you can help them.

If the bird's home tree is in your dog's pen, carefully move the babies to another tree no more than 30 feet away. If the nest is falling apart, put the whole thing in a small cardboard box and secure that in a nearby tree. If you move the babies into a box, try to use a plain box. If you use one that's exceptionally large, brightly colored, or adorned with moving pieces it may be too scary and discourage the parents from coming back.

You can also move the nest if it's in another potentially dangerous place like an air conditioning or dryer vent. If you are planning to move the nest, make sure that you absolutely have to for the sake of the bird family. There's always a risk that the parent birds could orphan the babies if they become too frightened or if there's too much human involvement.

All of these suggestions may seem tedious and time-consuming, but by following them you're doing the best thing for the baby birds. The main thing you have to remember is that a parent bird is absolutely the best one for the job of bringing up these youngsters. It's possible for humans to raise them, but there's more of a chance that the birds will die.

One big reason for this is because of the amount of dedication it takes to raise a baby bird. First of all, you can't just feed a bird bread. Every species of bird has a very specific, nutritionally-balanced diet that he must be on to grow up healthy. It's nearly impossible as a human to simulate the type of food that a baby bird would get in the wild. If the birds don't get what they need, the results can be devastating.

I'll never forget a grossly-distorted crow that had to be euthanized because of a horrible diet. A man had found the crow as a baby, fallen from the nest. He took him home and tried to raise him as best as he could for a few weeks, feeding him bread and water. It was only then that he realized something was drastically wrong and he brought the crow to the sanctuary.

The crow was almost fully feathered, but his legs were twisted and distorted. A careful exam by our medical director revealed bad news. The crow had not received a nutritionally proper diet for the past few weeks. He didn't get the calcium, for one, that he needed and his bones would never recover from that. Since the crow would not ever walk or fly, we chose to euthanize him to put him out of his misery. It was a very unfortunate situation because if the man had just returned the bird to the parent, he would have had a chance at a normal life like the rest of his species. This is a situation that wildlife rehabilitators see often.

The second reason why humans usually can't do as good of a job of raising wild birds as the parents is because most baby birds usually have to be fed as often as every 15 minutes from dawn until dusk. Even if you had the perfectly balanced diet for the bird, do you have time to break every 15 minutes of your day to feed a screaming baby?

Here's more incentive not to keep a wild bird: it's illegal. You have to have the proper license from your state wildlife agency to keep a wild animal, even a little baby bird. Many species are protected by both your state government and the federal government.

This is quite a bit of information to digest! To keep it simple, keep one thing in mind: baby birds are rarely orphaned. Basically, don't bring any of them into captivity unless you know for certain that the parent bird has died. Even then, remember that raising baby birds is often a two-parent job, and the one that's living will take over raising the babies if the other has died.

The only other time you should get a baby bird to a licensed wildlife rehabilitator is if the baby bird is obviously injured; for example, if he has a broken wing or leg, or perhaps if a dog or a cat has gotten hold of him and he has puncture wounds. A bird could also be in dire need of help from a rehabilitation center if he is bleeding profusely, paralyzed, or if he is dehydrated, evidenced by signs of lethargy, dry or loose skin, and sunken eyes. Sometimes a baby will have a head or neck injury. You can usually tell when this is the case if the baby's head is tilted abnormally to one side, or if he has jerky, rapid head and eye movements. If you're unsure if he needs help, call and ask.

If you end up taking a baby bird to a wildlife rehabilitator, put the baby in a dark cardboard box with tissue on the bottom for bedding. Try to keep the environment quiet, similar to a situation he'd find in nature. Birds don't relax to soft music and it can stress them if you gently stroke them to calm them down. Remember that birds don't get this type of treatment in the wild, and since they're not accustomed it, it'll generally cause them more stress than relaxation. Try to also keep household pets away from the box. Mammals are predators and they'll also stress the bird.

Keep the baby bird warm by placing a heating pad on low temperature halfway under the box. Separate the box and the heating pad with a towel so it doesn't get too hot. By putting the heating pad halfway under the box, you give the bird the option of moving to a cooler section if he gets too hot. A heating pad is the best option; putting the bird under a heat lamp or light bulb can damage or burn his delicate skin and cause dehydration.

Don't put any food or water in the box with the baby, especially water. These little guys don't know how to drink on their own yet, and they can actually drown in a small, shallow dish of water by losing their balance and falling into it. These little birds often don't know how, or even have the strength, to get out of a dangerous situation like that.

There's a better way to hydrate and feed baby birds. If the bird is opening his mouth, begging for food, a good temporary filler is dry dog or cat food soaked in water. Soak the pieces until they fluff up.

Then, break off tiny pieces with a tweezers and gently put them into the bird's open mouth one by one. Do this until the bird stops opening his mouth. There's enough moisture in the soaked food to supply the bird with water as well as nutrition. Actual droplets of water can be too much for little birds and they can drown or choke on them.

Don't force the bird to eat. If the bird doesn't seem interested in food, try gently tapping the side of the bird's beak with a tweezers. Sometimes this will encourage the bird to begin begging for food. Some species of birds like doves, however, don't eat that way. Instead, they reach into the parent bird's mouth themselves and eat regurgitated food. Only a licensed rehabilitator with training should feed birds like this because it requires a special technique. Do not feed injured birds at all. They're too weak and food or water can asphyxiate them.

Stick to the soaked cat food or dog food until the bird has reached his destination at the wildlife sanctuary or rehabilitation center. Cat and dog food is nutritionally a good temporary food. Things like milk or crackers are horrible for these youngsters and can make them sick. After all, milk comes from cows, which are mammals. Birds aren't mammals, and shouldn't be drinking milk at all!

Once the baby bird is safe and sound at a wildlife sanctuary, you might be curious as to how he's doing, wondering whatever happened to him. Although most sanctuaries or rehabilitation centers aren't open to the public for regular visitation, most welcome phone calls from people wanting to know how the situation turned out with the animal that they brought in, and caretakers often will have an update for you. Some places actually hold public releases, inviting people to watch wildlife being released back into their natural environment. It's worth it to check out your options. Good news on your animal will make all of your efforts feel worthwhile and rewarded.

Here is a summary of this chapter's advice:

- put a grounded baby bird back in the nest
- if you can't reach the nest use a makeshift nest
- put bird in cardboard box with tissues on the bottom
- secure in branch closest to nest
- or secure in tree nearby
- watch from distance for reunion
- remember that some species nest on ground
- identify such species in a bird book
- take baby bird to rehabilitator if parents are dead
- take baby bird to rehabilitator if injured

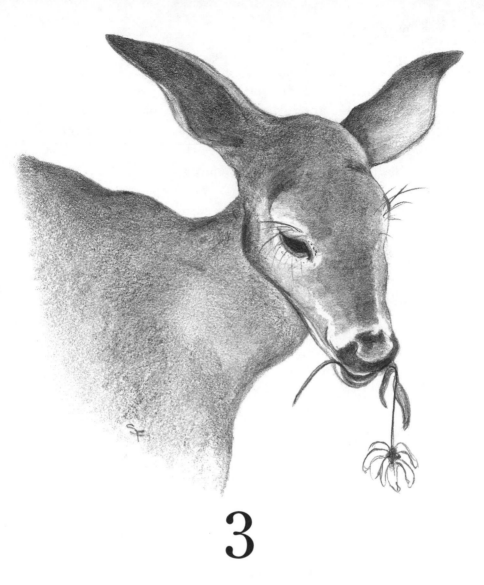

3

Growing the Deer-Resistant Garden

Snails used to ravish our flowers and other ornamental plants when my family lived in California, making it difficult to grow much of anything. I was too young at the time to remember much of that, but my mother remembers. That's why she was alarmed to see the same thing happening after we moved to Colorado.

Her joy over seeing healthy green shoots protrude through the rich mulch in her garden would turn to horror soon after they had broken through the ground's surface. Before they even had time to roll out leaves or blossom flowers, these shoots would turn into nothing more than gnawed-off stems.

My mother thought the culprits must be snails. It was an odd conclusion to come to, because she didn't think there was a problem with snails in Colorado. Sure enough, one early morning as dawn crept across the sky, she found out that her theory was wrong. The culprit that morning was standing in her garden, not creeping along leaving a trail of slime. He was a young buck taking a fancy to petunias.

The young buck came as a bit of a surprise. He was something we didn't expect to see in our neighborhood full of sidewalks, paved roads, and elementary schools. But our development was built in miles of foothills full of scrub oak, pine trees, and grassy clearings— areas once roamed by herds and herds of mule deer.

While some deer may have wandered away from these developments to live in the shrinking wildlands, many chose to stay. It has been quite easy for deer to become accustomed to our roadways, sidewalks, and the landscape we create from sod, different varieties of rock, and gardens—especially the gardens. Many of the beautiful ornamental plants and garden vegetables we love to grow have become the favorite foods of our neighborhood deer.

The deer aren't shy about picking and choosing what they want to eat. In fact, they'll roam from house to house, nibbling on their favorite plants at each place. They'll eat anything from trees and bushes to potted plants on your patio. My parents even have deer at their house that have learned how to walk up and down the concrete patio steps to get to their favorite potted annuals. Unless you have a fence over eight feet high that a deer might not be able to jump or an electric fence, or unless you don't mind if the deer eat your plants, you're going to have to come up with a plan to protect your gardens and plants from deer.

One way to combat deer-pruning is to plant things that they don't like to eat. There are several ornamentals that deer won't touch. You can strategically plant them around your yard, creating a sort of scent barrier that the deer won't want to cross. You can hide the more deer-desirable plants within that scent barrier. Deer rely on their sense of smell to find things that are safe and desirable. If you plant a wide variety of plants with strong odors, it'll confuse the deer and cause them to wander off to other areas where they can identify what they're eating.

Deer won't normally eat toxic and medicinal plants. They don't like plants with coarse, tough, hairy, sticky, or prickly leaves, and those plants that contain milky, sticky, or sappy substances. They also don't like plants with a lemon, mint, or herbal fragrance. Some deer-resistant plants include serviceberry, chokecherry, hawthorn, currant, sumac, elder, and rose. Through my own personal experiments, I've found, for example, that deer don't like catnip, catmint, mint, lemonbalm, snapdragons, sunflowers, purple robe, marigolds, alyssum, or parsley.

Deer, like this mule deer doe and her youngster, often eat up every green shoot in sight after surviving a winter with few edible options.

It's difficult to guarantee that a deer won't eat a certain type of plant, however. In the spring, after the deer have spent a long winter eating tree bark, twigs, and any other food they can find, they'll be ravenously hungry, eating most everything that begins to come up. This is the time when the plants will be the most tender and nutritious. Even in the summer when the plants are mature, a starving deer will eat most anything. If you don't have much to eat in your area at all, a deer will take whatever he can get. Much of your success will depend on the situation in your area.

Many nurseries, local agriculture extension offices, and local state wildlife offices can offer you help. They've done research and know more about the patterns of your local deer. Some of these places have lists of plants and other vegetation that deer don't like to eat, including native plants. It may be worth your time to research this before you spend any money on seeds or foliage. If the deer do take a few bites out of your shrubs or trees, the bright side may be that it'll just promote vigorous, new growth, just like any pruning you may do!

Regardless of what you plant, you're going to have foliage that you need to protect. There are many ways to do this. One traditional and inexpensive method is to hang bags of human hair around the plants you wish to protect. You can usually get human hair by inquiring at a local barber shop or beauty salon—there's plenty of hair there that just goes to waste! Try to get hair that hasn't been washed yet. There's more human scent in unwashed hair, and that human scent is what will scare the deer away. Put the hair in old nylon stockings or mesh bags and string them along a cord so that they're three for four feet apart. You may have to experiment with the dimensions.

Experimenting is the name of the game in my parents' neighborhood. Walking through it is like walking through a trade show. Most everyone has a nice display of beautiful flowers, and most everyone who has beautiful flowers has a method for keeping the deer away. You'll see anything from creative chicken wire covers protecting flower beds to bars of soap in the ground. Yes, bars of soap.

My dad was taking a walk one day when a particularly beautiful flower garden caught his eye. He noticed many of the same flowers in the bed that he had planted in his own yard, only his flowers had been eaten by the deer. He asked the neighbor what she did to keep the deer away. She invited him to take a closer look, and there in the ground along the base of all the flowers were slices of Irish Spring soap, a brand of soap with a particularly strong scent. This woman put the slices around her flowers in the spring, and said they lasted most of the summer. Soap is cheap, and it can work.

If you can't ward away the deer with stinky stuff, you can try scaring them away. Deer tend to be rather flighty creatures and it doesn't take much to frighten them. You can try putting pinwheels in the garden. The slightest breeze will provoke a flashy spin and a curious hum that most deer won't want to investigate!

Scare balloons can also be effective. You can get these at major garden centers or in gardening catalogs. They're inflatable balloons, often with bright colors and large faces—things that are unfamiliar in nature and can frighten wild animals. You should move these things around to different parts of the yard or garden from time to time, however, so that the deer don't become too accustomed to them.

During my research to find out what types of things are out there to deter deer, I came across an unusual gadget that might be one of the scariest things of all to a deer! It's a motion-activated sprinkler called "The Scarecrow," made by a company called Contech, Intelligent Animal Control (see Resources section in this book). It looks like a really ugly bird head, stuck on the end of a stake that goes into the ground. You connect a garden hose to the bottom of the stake. Whenever this device detects motion with its sensor, it triggers the sprinkler on top of the bird's head to shoot out water!

You can also try protecting your plants with netting and chicken wire. Try putting tubes of Vexar netting around individual seedlings to cut back on damage to trees. This material degrades in sunlight and will be gone in several years. You can also wrap specific plants in chicken wire or netting, expanding the enclosures as the plants get bigger. There's also special netting designed to drape over trees, shrubs, and small plants to protect them from wildlife.

Electric fencing can be very effective at keeping deer out of your garden as well. Check with your local zoning department to make sure that this is permitted in your area. If neighborhood covenants allow, an eight-foot-high fence is recommended. That's usually high enough to keep deer out of the area.

If you're not too crazy about having scarecrows, pinwheels, and balloons all over your yard, that's understandable. It could begin to look like a toy store. There's good news if you're looking for a less-visible way to repel deer.

There are plenty of concoctions you can create to spray on your plants to keep deer from eating them. Commercial repellents are already made up for you. There are contact repellents that you spray directly on the plants to keep deer from eating them, and there are area repellents that you place in the troubled areas. The latter repel deer by emitting a foul odor. These repellents are available at most gardening stores. The important thing to remember is that these products have to be continually re-applied, especially after rain.

More extreme methods include buying coyote urine. There are companies that sell it and some people say it's effective. Some local zoos will also allow you to buy lion manure, which some gardeners like to use. I've even heard of people using their own urine in their gardens to ward off deer.

Concoctions you can mix at home include a spray of 20 percent whole eggs and 80 percent water. You can remove the white membrane to help the egg mix better with the water. Spray this mixture on the plants you wish to protect; it's usually good for about a month.

A hot sauce mixture is effective. You can either use Tabasco sauce or cayenne pepper, mixed with water in a 50/50 solution. You can also use ground habanero peppers, mixed one part to nine parts water. Deer don't like hot sauce on their food and won't eat anything that tastes this way. You can also sprinkle cayenne pepper on the ground in areas where you're expecting seedlings. Again, you'll have to reapply these mixtures after heavy watering or rain. If you use a

Different types of peppers are irritating to a deer's nose. If pepper is on your plants, that deer will most likely look elsewhere for a meal!

great deal of cayenne pepper, keep in mind that it's very irritating to an animal's eyes, nose, and feet. If you have pets, try to keep them out of those areas to protect them. You may also want to experiment with the spicy stuff by spraying a small amount on one leaf to see how the plant reacts. Some of the hot sauces can damage the leaves. In that case, spray it around the plants.

Most of this research has been put to the test in my family's gardens. We have a large vegetable garden and six separate flower beds. My dad always used commercial repellents, like "Not Tonight Deer," which he says works well. But I still noticed that deer seemed to nibble on different plants here and there.

One year in particular, I seeded all six flower beds and the garden myself, investing a great deal of time and money. I was trying to fill most of the six flower beds with perennials so they would come up year after year on their own, saving us planting time and money in the future. With that kind of an investment on the line, I wanted to make sure the deer wouldn't eat the plants, let alone step foot in the gardens. I had heard that gardeners swear by blood meal, so I decided to give that a try.

Blood meal is a fertilizer for plants, so it can help them grow while it's repelling deer. I generously sprinkled it in all of the flower beds and the garden and waited to see what happened. It seems this blood meal did the trick. Not only did the deer avoid all of the plants, but they rarely even set foot in any of the garden areas (I sprinkled it around the perimeters of the gardens to make them smell unpleasant). Just to be safe, I applied the blood meal about once every two to three weeks.

During this time, I also used bone meal, which seems to be effective too. Other gardeners recommend using Milorganite or feathermeal. You can get all of these items at local garden centers. Take the time to read the directions on the bags, however. It's important to note that you should only sprinkle some of these substances around the base of the plants and not on the leaves because they can burn the leaves. You may also want to read the instructions to find out if it's safe to use these things in your vegetable garden or on your edible plants.

This all may seem like quite a bit of work, and you may be wondering if there's an easier way. Some people say there is, that solving this problem is as easy as getting a large dog.

Deer are extremely frightened of dogs and if you have one in your yard, it's almost a guarantee that you won't have any deer. If you do decide to get a dog, make sure that you really want a dog as well. The dog will need food, water, shelter, attention, veterinary care, etc. If you're not willing to properly care for the dog, it might not be a good idea to get one.

If you do get a dog, let him naturally deter the deer by barking or scurrying around the yard. Don't set the dog loose on the deer. This can greatly stress the deer, causing him to run into traffic or another dangerous situation. Also, a dog could seriously injure a deer if he got hold of one. Often, this causes the deer a great deal of suffering, and occasionally an agonizing death. Fawns are commonly attacked by dogs. Dogs can easily kill these little creatures and it's important to monitor the situation closely to make sure your dog doesn't capture a deer.

It could also be against city or county ordinances to let your dog off a leash. This could result in fines or your dog being picked up by local animal control officers. Some states also have laws that make it illegal for a dog to harass wildlife. In the state of Colorado, dogs can be impounded for this, and violators can face stiff fines. By law, a citizen or a peace officer can legally destroy a dog for harassing wildlife.

One last thing to keep in mind if you get a dog is to be mindful of your neighbors. If the dog is barking for hours on end, a neighbor could call the police, and even take you to court over a nuisance dog. Dogs require a great deal of responsibility, and the choice to get one should be well thought-out.

No matter what choice you make, try to have patience and try to experiment with the above suggestions. Deer are creatures of habit. They often return to the same places day after day to eat and sleep. If your yard is part of a deer's daily routine, it may take that deer awhile to break the pattern and learn to feed elsewhere. Eventually, you will find a solution, perhaps one that allows you to enjoy both these beautiful creatures and your gardens at the same time.

Here is a summary of this chapter's advice:

- put human hair around plants
- put slices of smelly soap around plants
- use spicy mixtures or cayenne pepper around plants
- scatter blood meal, bone meal, or feather meal
- use commercial sprays
- cover plants with netting or chicken wire
- install scare balloons
- install a motion-activated sprinkler
- build an eight-foot-high fence

- build an electric fence
- plant vegetation deer don't like
- research at local cooperative extension

4

There's a Cardinal Knocking on My Window

The cardinal was beating his head against the window so hard, that he was leaving tiny drops of blood in some places. The woman who owned the house was convinced this bird was trying to get in to attack her. She said this bird seemed to follow her from room to room, beating his head against all of the windows.

The woman panicked. She even thought the bird was possessed. I thought at first that this had to be a prank call, but as she screamed on and on, I realized this was indeed a real situation!

I'll admit that I didn't know what to tell her. This was the first time I had taken a call like this at the sanctuary, and I had to put the woman on hold and ask my boss, the wildlife expert and veteran rehabilitator, what to do.

I found out that the cardinal was only trying to protect his territory. This was a male cardinal and he chose this woman's yard as his place to mate and nest. Each time the cardinal got near the woman's home, he would see his own reflection in her windows. He was interpreting this as another male cardinal in his territory, and he was attacking the windows to try and drive him away. What he didn't understand was that he was just attacking his own reflection.

Cardinals, like many other species of birds, are very territorial. In order to fix this temporary problem, the woman was going to have to find a way to break up the reflection in the windows. We told her she could do this by putting towels or newspapers over the windows so that the cardinal would no longer see himself. Another option was to pull down the shades, close the blinds, or pull curtains across the windows. We also told her she could try putting a bright light in front of the window. All of these things will help break up the reflection. If you're not sure if that's happening, go outside and check. You may have to alter the outsides of your windows temporarily.

Some of the suggestions may sound like gaudy solutions, but they're not forever. This type of behavior is typical of mating season and won't last a long time. It could be interesting for you to watch the entire process. Mating season goes hand in hand with a nest full of baby birds. Whether one parent does the job, or two parents care for the babies together, you'll most likely have the opportunity to watch a family of birds grow up and fly from their nest to adulthood. It's very much like having kids of your own!

However, not everyone wants birds nesting around their home. Oftentimes, the nests are in very peculiar places, and they could be in dangerous situations for baby birds if the parents choose to raise a family in an area that has cats or dogs.

Birds have become, like other wildlife, quite accustomed to nesting in our yards and around our homes. They're not shy. They'll build nests in your chimneys, above your doorways, and in your hanging plants. In fact, at my parents' house, a pair of nesting house finches have decided that they like my dad's choice of hanging plants. Every year, he buys a hanging geranium mix, potted in a nice moss basket. For the past couple of years, this pair of house finches has built a nest right in the middle of the geranium. That way it's hidden by big, sprawling leaves and red flowers. The plant doesn't always fare so well after that, but it's exciting to watch the female lay her little blue eggs and hatch babies.

If baby birds are the last thing you want hanging outside your window, there are some things you can do to try to make your home an unpleasant choice for nesting birds before the baby season even starts.

Start by checking the perimeter of your home or business. Prevent nesting in your chimney by capping it, and put screens or netting over dryer vents and roof gutters, other popular places for nests. Check the outside of your home for loose boards that may have given way to holes, nooks, or crannies that birds may find appealing. Plug all small holes with caulking or wood filler; you can even cover holes with wire screening or fill them in with steel wool or another type of plug. Replace any other loose panels, shingles, and siding.

Once you've checked the perimeter and made any necessary repairs to potential nest sites, there are some things that you can do to try to keep birds from scouting out the area entirely. Try putting scare balloons in the area. These are balloons with big eyes and scary faces that may frighten birds away and keep them from hanging around. Strips of foil, pinwheels, and other flashy devices like these will also frighten birds. Place them in areas where you don't want them. Move them from time to time so that the birds don't become too accustomed to them and realize that they won't harm them.

Other good deterrents are owl decoys or rubber snakes. The owl decoy is scary to small birds because some large birds of prey like the owl will eat smaller birds. Snakes are also predators so rubber impostors may frighten birds away. Again, you'll have to move these decoys from time to time so that the birds don't get too used to them.

You can usually pick up these items through gardening catalogs, in nurseries, and even through advertisements in some wildlife magazines. There's also information available on the Internet.

As you're trying to keep birds from nesting around your home, you may happen to come across a nest full of baby birds. If at all possible, try to leave the nest and the babies, allowing the parents to finish raising them before you bird-proof the area for good. It only takes a few weeks for baby birds to grow feathers and fly off. It's best to try and wait for this to happen because any type of human involvement will risk the parents abandoning the babies. Once the babies have grown up and are gone, you can modify that nesting site so the birds won't nest there anymore.

If the baby birds are in immediate danger—perhaps a repair man is coming to fix holes and board things up and there's no way it can wait—you can move the nest. Gently take it and secure it well in the closest tree, something no more than 30 feet away. The parent birds will usually resume care. If the nest falls apart, you can put the babies in a small cardboard box with tissue on the bottom and relocate the makeshift nest to a nearby tree (you may want to read over chapter 2 to learn more about baby birds and their stages of development).

If you're still attracting birds, even after modifying your home or business and using scare tactics, take a look around and ask yourself what you might be doing to attract birds. There may be trash exposed in the area. That will attract some species of birds. Be sure to keep covers on trash cans and don't leave food scraps lying around.

Pet food could also be your problem. Some species of birds, such as different types of jays and magpies, are big fans of cat and dog food. They'll fill up their beaks with several pieces at a time, fly off, eat them, and return for more. If you're feeding your pet outside you might want to consider feeding that pet inside so that you stop attracting these birds. If a bird finds a solid food source in your area and likes the nesting opportunities, he'll be more likely to pick a mate and nest at your house!

Are you putting out food to attract a particular species of bird? Perhaps a favorite songbird? If you are, it's almost inevitable that you're going to attract other species of birds to the area whether you want to or not. It's not very feasible to expect that you'll attract just the colorful birds, or a particular species that you'd like to see.

The same thing goes for bird houses. You may be trying to attract one species in particular by putting up a bird house, but chances are, you'll wind up with several other species of birds checking out or nesting in this nice, manufactured home. Many people put up purple martin houses and end up with a bunch of sparrows for residents.

You can modify this situation a little bit. For example, any boxes with holes larger that one inch in diameter will attract birds like sparrows and starlings. If you want to attract only smaller birds like chickadees, the solution is to use boxes with holes smaller than one inch in diameter.

If you don't have a problem with nesting birds, you may have a problem with loitering birds, or birds who just use your house or place of business as a place to hang out. Once again, there are a few things you can try to discourage birds from doing this.

Bird netting can be used to prevent roosting on window ledges, rafters, and other horizontal surfaces. Stretch the netting across the surface where you don't want birds. It is also helpful for sealing off any openings where birds may want to perch or nest. They don't like bird netting very much because it's hard for them to stand on it. You can also use this netting on fruit or nut trees, vegetable crops, and grapevines. It'll keep birds away and prevent them from eating the goods.

You can also try bird spikes to keep birds from hanging around. These are panels of spikes that you can place along ledges or windowsills. Obviously, the spikes are all but impossible to land on. You can also roll up small sheets of chicken wire and secure the rolls to the places where you don't want birds.

Flat surfaces, like ledges, can be turned into false ledges that are difficult to perch on. A false ledge can be made by adhering masonry, metal, or wood at an angle of more than 60 degrees over the original ledge. Birds will slip off when they land and will most likely find another place to perch.

If birds aren't perching or nesting, you may also notice they're drumming—drumming against the side of your home or business, that is! Woodpeckers are notorious for this. They'll drum against anything from metal gutters to wooden siding. Woodpeckers have sharp, chisel-like bills which they use for drilling and digging into things, mainly trees. They cling to the bark with the strong claws on their feet and use their stiff tails as props as they're doing this. Most species of woodpeckers will nest in the holes they create in the trees, or in some type of cavity they might find in a stump or a tree limb.

Loitering birds, like these rock doves or pigeons, are often unwanted at businesses and homes.

Woodpeckers may peck at the siding or your house, however, especially if it has soft or rotting wood. One way to discourage the hammering or drumming is to cover the surface they're pecking with foam or fabric. Check the siding on your house or business, and plug up any small holes that a woodpecker might notice and peck to make larger. Sometimes, woodpeckers will drill to find food. If you have a consistent problem with woodpeckers, it may be that your wood is infested with insects. To solve the problem, you'll have to treat the wood to get rid of them.

If you have many woodpeckers in the area that are all drumming against your house, it can actually be helpful to put up a nest box for one pair of these birds. Sometimes what happens when one pair takes up residence near your home is that they'll become very territorial and drive all of the other woodpeckers away.

If you hear a single, loud bang against your house, it may not be a woodpecker you have to worry about, but an injured bird. If you have large, clear windows, you may already know what I'm talking about—birds flying into those windows.

The sound is unique, and unfortunately, sickening. It sounds like someone throwing a snowball against your window, a distinct "boom" that often means a bird didn't notice the window and flew right into it. This is a very common problem. Birds don't often see glass and end up temporarily knocking themselves out or killing themselves. To the birds, the glass is an open space that they think they can fly right on through!

You can help prevent birds from doing this by making them notice the glass. One good way to do this is to put a black plastic silhouette of a large bird or hawk in the window. These can be found in wildlife magazines, bird specialty stores, and sometimes home improvement stores. You stick the silhouette to the outside of your window. Birds will see this and shy away from the glass. If you don't want to use a bird silhouette, you can use something else to make them notice the window like strips of tape.

If a bird does fly into your window, you may be able to help him. Pick him up and put him in a dark cardboard box. This way, you'll get the unconscious bird off of the ground and out of danger of being eaten by a cat or another predator. Put some tissue on the bottom of the box so the bird has something to grip onto. Then, put the box in a dark, quiet place for awhile. The bird may be knocked out and just need some time to regain consciousness. The best case scenario is that the bird will wake up again and be well enough to fly off. If it's not too cold outside, you can also put the bird under a bush in the shade to try and recover. Be sure to keep all pets out of the area if you do this.

Check on the bird after 30 minutes or so. If the bird is standing up and appears alert and not injured, take the box outside, open it, and give him a chance to fly away again. If the bird is unable to fly, he may have head trauma or an injured wing. Put the bird back in the cardboard box with ventilation holes and contact a local wildlife rehabilitation center that can treat the bird for head trauma or mend his broken wind. A bird with head trauma is in critical condition and needs continuous care to recover.

If the bird doesn't regain consciousness, his neck may be broken. This is the worse case scenario and one that is all too common. Birds can instantaneously break their necks when they hit a window. Leave the bird in the cardboard box for some time, an hour or so. If the bird never regains consciousness or stands up, and if the body begins to stiffen, the bird is dead. If you're unsure, get the bird to a wildlife rehabilitation center.

If birds aren't flying into your windows, they may be flying through your windows or your open doors. This is another common scenario, especially with businesses. Birds will accidentally fly inside a home or a business and become trapped.

If a bird is trapped in a small area, the best thing to do is to open the window and the screen. The bird will usually fly out. If it's dark outside, open the window and screen, but turn on a bright light outside. The bird will fly toward the light and the fresh air. Close blinds or drapes covering windows that you won't or can't open. This will keep the bird from flying into them. If you're uncomfortable doing any of this, contact a local licensed wildlife rehabilitation center or your local division of wildlife for help.

If a bird is trapped in a large area, like a warehouse, you can turn off all the lights and open the doors to the outside. This can be done at dark as well, but make sure the outside lights are turned on. Just like moths, birds will fly toward the light to get out.

You can also try to get birds out of a large area like a store or a warehouse by putting a spread of food, like seeds, just outside the door. If the bird gets hungry enough, the food will draw him toward the outside of the building. It may take time. Just keep feeding the bird or birds by the door before they figure out that they can fly outside. Try to get him in the habit of eating by the door, especially when people aren't around or during low traffic times. Eventually, the bird should fly back outside.

People are one obstacle that often stand in the way of a bird flying back into the wild. Obviously, a business will be quite busy with people coming and going all the time. Birds are generally quite frightened of people and won't go near the door if people are coming in and out.

If a bird is trapped in your business, you may want to try to help him right after closing when he won't be as frightened and when he'll be more likely to fly toward the seeds and the outside. This would also be the best time to turn out all the lights, giving the bird a chance to fly toward the outside light. If you have automatic doors, find a way to keep the doors open for a period of time until the bird has safely found his way out. If this doesn't work, contact a wildlife rehabilitation center or your local division of wildlife. They may have a technique they use to help trapped birds.

Experiences with birds don't have to be like something out of an Alfred Hitchcock movie! There are usually ways to resolve these problems and to help you learn to live with them. If you ever have a cardinal knocking at your window, perhaps now you'll breathe a sigh of relief. Perhaps now you'll have a better understanding of bird behavior and begin to have hope that there is a way to better coexist.

Here is a summary of this chapter's advice:

- break reflections in windows
- cap chimney and vents
- replace loose siding or shingles on roof
- install scare balloons
- set up an owl decoy
- apply strips of foil
- place rubber snakes in areas where you want to discourage birds
- bring in pet food, water
- cover trash and compost
- use bird netting on vegetable garden or fruit trees
- use bird spikes on ledges
- use rolls of chicken wire on ledges
- create false or angled ledges
- be aware that a specific bird food may attract all birds
- be aware that specific bird houses may attract many species

5

Leave Bambi in the Forest

From the moment the big, burly hunter stepped out of his car he caught my eye. Here was a tall, muscular man carrying a tiny, spotted fawn in his arms. I knew right away this was the hunter whom I had spoken to earlier. He was very troubled over a situation with a fawn and didn't know what to do.

He was sure the fawn was abandoned. The man was working with a construction crew, clearing undeveloped wildlands to prepare the area for a large office building that was going to be built. One evening as he was leaving work, he noticed a fawn wandering around and looking disoriented. The little guy was at the edge of the field they had just cleared. The man guessed that the bulldozers had disrupted the fawn and scared off the mother. He was probably right.

The man knew already to leave the fawn alone in the area where he found him. He knew that the mother may be nearby, ready to return for the fawn at any time. He left the fawn there overnight. But the next day, the man found the fawn in the same spot, still wandering around and looking disoriented.

The fawn looked weaker than he had the previous evening. The mother was nowhere in sight. The man continued to work throughout the day, all the while keeping an eye on this little guy. When it was time to go home that evening, the man picked up the fawn and brought him home.

The man found his own actions baffling. He told me he didn't know why he felt the need to save this fawn. He said he had hunted deer all of his life, and that, logically, it made no sense for him to try and save this one's life—a life that may be taken by a hunter some day anyway. He did say, however, that he somehow felt responsible for this abandoned fawn since he was part of the crew that disrupted his home and scared away his mother. It's very likely that the constant commotion is what continuously scared the doe away, causing her to become so frightened that she never returned. For that reason, he saved this fawn's life.

The man said not only was he baffled by the fact that he saved this fawn's life, he was baffled by how attached he had become to the little guy! He immediately named the fawn "Buddy" and tied a little red and white handkerchief around his neck. The man took an old beer bottle, put a rubber nipple used for feeding calves on the end, and began feeding the fawn goat's milk. He then called Wildlife Rescue for help.

The man wanted the best for Buddy, and he knew that entailed getting him to a wildlife sanctuary where he could be raised with other fawns, fed nutritionally balanced formulas, and given around-the-clock care. He just never knew that he was going to miss his little Buddy as much as he did!

He carried the little fawn in his arms and brought him into our visitor's center. He didn't want to let Buddy go. He asked me if he could feed him one last time. I told him "of course," prepared some formula for him in his beer bottle, and left the two of them alone. After he was done feeding the fawn, he poked his head around the corner and said, "I'm ready."

The man patted the fawn on the head as I took him from him. He had no words at first, but then turned to me as he was leaving and said: "You know, I've been a hunter all my life. I've hunted and killed deer. But after spending time with this little guy, I know that I will never be able to hunt again." As those last words came out, a tear appeared.

You don't have to be on a construction crew to find a fawn. While construction and developments commonly displace and disrupt wildlife, it's very likely you'll find a fawn in other situations. You may find one while taking a stroll through the woods. You may find one quietly lying in your yard one morning when you wake up. You may even find a distressed fawn near a dead doe off the highway. There are many situations you could find yourself in, and it happens all too often that well-meaning people pick up fawns to try to save them. Often, they don't need saving, but there are signs you can look for to help you know the difference.

The way a doe cares for a fawn is very different from how a human would care for a baby. While our babies are in our care most of the day and night, a doe will often go off to feed and leave her fawn unattended for hours at a time. This happens for the fawn's first week or so of life. After the fawn is born, he's usually too weak to follow his mother around. That's why she'll leave him bedded down in brush or even in open fields while she goes off to feed. She'll return to her baby to let him nurse, often moving him from time to time so he's not always in the same spot.

The mother does this for the fawn's own safety. By leaving him behind, she hides and protects him against predators during his weak

Does, like this mule deer doe, will leave their newborn fawns for hours at a time while they go off to eat.

time. Once he's stronger, he can run and better fend for himself. After the fawn has grown stronger, he will soon begin to follow his mom. He'll basically remain with her until he's old enough to go off on his own.

It's most likely that you'll stumble across fawns while they're in this stage. They're usually lying down with their heads tucked against their bodies. They hold very still so that predators won't notice them. This is one of their best defenses, aside from their spots, which help camouflage them. This is why a fawn will usually not move as you approach.

Newborn fawns, in general, appear very frail, scared, and vulnerable. It's very tempting to want to pick them up and save them because they seem so unprotected nestled in the grass or bushes by themselves. The reality is, however, that the fawns are usually fine and should be left in the exact spots where they're found! Their mothers will be back soon to let them nurse.

Sometimes, if you get too close to a fawn, you could startle him. The fawn may get up and take off running. This can be a very dangerous situation for the fawn. Predators could notice him and attack. He could also become disoriented and lost after leaving the place where his mother put him. If he's in a suburban-type area, he could even run into traffic, fences, or into pens with dogs and become injured or killed. It's best to try and keep your distance. If you want to monitor the fawn, watch from someplace nearby.

There's nothing wrong with keeping an eye on the situation. A good rule of thumb to try and determine whether or not a fawn is truly abandoned is to give the situation 24 hours. Leave the fawn where you found him and watch from a place where you won't frighten the mother when she does come back. You can even leave the area and return 24 hours later to see if the fawn is still there.

Does generally move their fawns to new spots day to day. If you return to the same area 24 hours later and the fawn is gone, that's a good sign. It most likely means the mother has come to get her baby and he's fine. If the fawn is in the exact same spot where he was the day before, it could be a sign that the fawn is abandoned.

There's always the remote possibility that the mother just left her baby in the same spot. But it could also be that she never came back for one reason or another. You have a few options at this point. You can monitor the situation for a bit longer to see if the mother comes back. You can also call your local division of wildlife or a wildlife rehabilitator to get advice on what to do. They can help you monitor the situation and can give you professional guidance.

There are some stronger signs of an abandoned fawn. One of them is if the fawn is standing up, wandering around aimlessly, and crying or bleating. This is usually a sign that the fawn is distressed and without a mother. Generally, that means the fawn needs help.

If you find a fawn with flies landing on an open wound, in his nostrils, or in the eyes, he's in need of help. These flies are usually an indication of a very sick fawn, and without help, he could soon be infested with maggots. If you see a fawn with small white fly eggs on him, contact a wildlife rehabilitation center. Describe the situation and ask for help. It may be that the fawn needs to come in for treatment.

This next situation will only happen in certain parts of the country, but if you find a fawn who is covered in fire ants, he's in need of immediate help. Fire ants are found in the southern region of the United States. These ants will actually crawl inside an animal's nose and mouth and begin to eat at the soft mucus membranes, sometimes traveling far down the esophagus toward the stomach. A fawn in this situation will need immediate treatment to help flush all of those ants out and to kill them. Often, fawns who have been attacked by fire ants are temporarily blind and will need several weeks of treatment to help them recover. Call for help.

A sure sign that a fawn has been abandoned is if you find him near his dead mother on or near the roadway. If you come across a dead doe and you're curious to know whether or not she left behind a fawn, check her nipples. If the doe was a nursing mother, her nipples will be large and pronounced, like an udder on a cow. You should be able to see that the areas around the nipples are swollen with milk. It would be a difficult task to find where a doe has hidden her fawn, but in this situation, there is most likely one out there who's now in need of help.

There are no hard and fast rules most of the time when it comes to determining whether or not a fawn is abandoned. It's important not to confuse a healthy fawn for an abandoned fawn. Newborn fawns will appear emaciated and weak. They're quite thin when they're born, and they wobble a bit as they're learning to walk. One way to tell the difference between a healthy fawn and a sickly fawn is by their appearance.

A healthy fawn will have a slick, shiny coat. This is a sign of a baby who is being regularly nursed, getting all of the nutrition and liquid that he needs. A fawn who has gone without food for a couple of days will begin to have rough-looking fur. This is a sign of dehydration. A sickly fawn may also have a crusty nose and eyes. Again, distressed fawns will generally wander aimlessly and cry aloud.

A fawn who obviously needs help is one who has a broken leg, a gunshot wound, or another type of obvious injury. Deer injure themselves quite often, but many of them can still get around all right with those injuries. In order for the fawn's injury to warrant taking him out of the wild to a rehabilitation center, it should be an injury that is clearly impairing him and keeping him from following his mother. Sometimes just taking a deer out of the wild causes him so much stress that it can kill him. A cut or a limp isn't worth the stress of taking a deer out of the wild. Often, they do a better job of healing themselves in their own environment than they do in ours.

There was a three-legged deer at the sanctuary that lives on as a legend. He's a good example how wild animals can often mend themselves better in their own environment. This particular deer came in with a dangling, broken leg. Aside from that injury, he was quite healthy and strong. While staying overnight in an outdoor recovery pen, he jumped the fence and escaped. He was still enclosed by the tall, 12-foot perimeter fence, but he was free to roam on 21 acres of Texas hill country. He obviously wanted to be free.

We didn't see this deer for awhile, but one day, he surfaced again. His grossly distorted leg, which couldn't have been saved anyway, had fallen off. He now only had three legs, but that didn't impair him in the least. He grazed, ran, frolicked. He had no signs of infection and the stump where his leg had fallen off was healed over. We saw this deer often for years. He became a sort of martyr for us.

If you find a sickly or injured fawn that can't follow his mother, or one by his dead mother, pick him up and call for help. A rehabilitation center is the best place for a fawn because it has the proper formulas and its staff often work with veterinarians who are familiar with how to treat wild animals. They'll also be able to raise the fawn with other deer. This will mean he'll be properly socialized and able to return to the wild someday, no longer depending on humans for care and food. It can be disastrous when people try to keep deer as pets.

People who try to raise fawns often feed them milk, which is the worst formula for them. This will cause them to get sick, have diarrhea, and sometimes dehydrate to the point of death. Fawns raised by humans will also never learn to fear them. If they're ever released back into the wild they often get into trouble by approaching the wrong humans who hurt them or kill them. Grown deer will often hurt people by rearing, kicking, and head-butting them in play. It's also illegal to keep a wild animal without the proper permits.

A situation in central Colorado turned tragic for a young elk who had become too friendly with humans.

The elk was apparently abandoned. A couple found the calf on their property one day. After that, the elk adopted the couple and the couple adopted the elk. The people took care of the elk and the elk hung around while she was growing up.

As the elk ventured off on her own, neighbors began to complain that she was a nuisance. The elk had no fear of people. They told wildlife officers that she would wander around on their property, sleep on their porches, and they said she was becoming bothersome. One neighbor reported she tried to walk into their house.

The situation took a turn for the worse when a family called 911 to report that the elk had attacked them as they were hiking on a pedestrian trail in a local campground. The Colorado Division of Wildlife took the stance that the elk had become dangerous. Officers said that an elk that size—300 pounds—could easily kill an adult. They also said the elk could be dangerous to young children who may come across her. The elk had become, according to the division, a threat to public safety.

The fatal day came when the sheriff's office received a call about an elk stopping traffic on a nearby highway. Officers responded and were ordered by a local wildlife officer to kill the elk. They did.

This event caused controversy and was discussed in the media statewide. The couple had felt the elk was a part of their family and insisted that wildlife officers could have taken other routes—including tranquilizing the elk and shipping her to a wildlife sanctuary or a zoo. The division simply calls this "a case for not domesticating our wildlife."

Although the above story is about an elk, a much larger animal than a deer, a deer's potential for this type of disaster is similar. Locating a rehabilitation center for a fawn in trouble is the best thing you can do for him.

There are some things you can do to make the fawn more comfortable if it's going to be awhile before you can get him to a wildlife rehabilitator.

The first thing is to not give the fawn cow's milk. Again, it has a different make-up than deer's milk and it can cause the fawn to become very sick. If you feel the fawn is dehydrated, you can give him some room-temperature, unflavored Pedialyte from a baby bottle. You can pick up Pedialyte in any grocery store in the baby food section. You may have to cut the nipple a bit to make the opening slightly larger. This will encourage the fawn to drink. Don't force the fawn to eat. He may be in shock or distress.

The second thing you can do to make the fawn more comfortable is to keep him in a dark, quiet environment. This will help to calm him down. When you're transporting the fawn to the rehabilitation center, try to use a large pet carrier. Cover the door with a towel, however, so that the fawn doesn't panic and try to get out. If you don't have a carrier, you can use a large cardboard box with air holes. Be sure to put an old towel or other bedding down on the bottom for the fawn.

It may be tempting to hold the fawn in your lap while you're transporting him, but this can be dangerous for you and the fawn. If the fawn were to become scared and bolt, you might have a car accident. The fawn could also get injured. The fawn will be calmer in a carrier or a box. You have to remember that the fawn doesn't recognize you as his parent. He may see you as a predator and be scared to be around you. This fawn just went from the wildlands to your home. That's a big change in environment!

The above situations are cases where the fawn needs to go to a rehabilitation center for help. But what if you've picked up a fawn by accident and now realize that he needs no help? Don't fret! There may still be hope that you can reunite that fawn with his mother. Your human scent generally isn't enough to deter the doe from resuming care of her baby.

You need to try to get the fawn back to the spot where you found him immediately. The longer you wait to return the fawn, the more likely it is that the doe will reject him. She may not return again at all if she's already tried to find the baby but can't. The longer you wait, the more you risk breaking the bond between the fawn and the doe. She'll be more likely to reject him after being away from him for several days.

The reunion process is similar to the 24-hour rule. Return the fawn to the same spot and try to get him bedded down. Make sure he doesn't try to follow you after you leave. He may have become attached to you in that short amount of time.

Give the reunion a good 24 hours. If the fawn has moved the next day, the mother probably came and got him. If the fawn is still there, you may have an abandoned fawn on your hands at that point. Call for help.

Some situations may require a little bit of your help temporarily. Often, a doe will bed down her fawn in the quiet, early-morning hours. The area she chose may seen quiet at the time, but by the time morning hits, the area may become busy.

Sometimes people find fawns in places like a neighborhood yard or a grassy area next to an apartment complex. The best thing to do is to try to leave the fawn where he is. However, if the fawn is in danger of being hit by traffic, or if it looks like he's becoming scared and may get up and run into traffic, you may need to contact a wildlife rehabilitator for help.

If the fawn has already gotten up and started walking around, disturbed somehow, try to relocate him to the cover of some nearby brush or tall grass where he won't be seen. Approach the fawn with a towel or a blanket to cover him. Try to bring another person with you for help in case the fawn tries to bolt. He may run into traffic and get hurt. When you get to him, put the towel or blanket over his head. This will keep him calm and keep him from struggling as you try to move him. Make sure the fawn is bedded down in the new area before you remove the towel and leave him. Try to only do this when it's absolutely necessary. If you're unsure, call you local division of wildlife for help.

A sanctuary gives a wild animal like a fawn a second chance at life. At Wildlife Rescue, there would be as many as 80 fawns at a time running and playing together in a large, grassy field we had set aside just for deer. The fawns had large trees to lie under, a shed for shelter, and tall grass to nestle down and sleep in. When you passed by the enclosure, often you would just see little fawn heads peering out from the tall brush.

The fawns were left to socialize and play with each other, never interacting with humans until it was feeding time. Even then, we would line up rows and rows of baby bottles filled with fawn formula and let them eat on their own. It doesn't take long for the fawns to grow and begin foraging for food independently. When the fawns are strong and old enough, they're gathered up in covered trailers and taken to secret release sites—often private property where no hunting is allowed—where they're set free.

It may not be the life they were supposed to lead, but when they leave the cover of the trailers, their injuries, abandonment—all of their individual tragedies—are left behind. Even fawns with terrible injuries that have left them without a rear leg do fine. When they've learned to balance on their other three legs, they run just as fast and are just as agile as the other deer. Due to people's efforts to rescue and return all of these fawns to a normal life, they have one once again.

Here is a summary of this chapter's advice:

- remember that does leave fawns for hours at a time
- observe fawn for 24 hours; if fawn is in same place, he could be abandoned
- if fawn is wandering and crying he could be abandoned
- fawns with seriously impairing injuries need a rehabilitator
- fawns with flies on open wounds may need a rehabilitator
- fawns with fire ants need a rehabilitator
- fawn next to dead doe on highway needs a rehabilitator

6

Lions and Tigers and Bears

There are many ghost towns in Colorado, deserted places with enough bits and pieces still standing to tell a story of an old way of life. However, one town just west of Canon City, Colorado, is a living replica of a ghost town that laid itself to rest in the 1860s.

Buckskin Joe Frontier Town and Railway is a place that recreates the old mining town called Buckskin Joe. It recaptures the spirit of the Old West in an actual frontier setting with 30 buildings that are original structures from ghost towns in the Rocky Mountain region. People come to learn about Colorado's history, as well as experience things like gunfights, hangings, and magic shows. Some of the entertainment is based on real events that happened in the 1800s.

Perhaps one event that the park didn't bank on having was an act by a guest who wasn't on the entertainment line-up. That guest was a black bear.

The bear had been frequenting the park in search of food. Wildlife officers say that food is the main reason a bear will initially come around and stay around. The park offered plenty of leftover snacks from all of its tourists.

The bear was causing trouble, however. He was getting into trash and searching the rest of the park for a meal or two. The Colorado Division of Wildlife stepped in after the bear had come around one too many times and set a trap. The bear found himself in that trap soon afterwards.

The policy at the time offered the bear one last chance. The bear would be tagged, tattooed, and relocated to a remote area where he wouldn't be around humans. The hope was that he would return to a way of life where he relied solely on nature for his needs rather than humans. However, if the bear ever found his way back to the park, he would be destroyed.

This two-strikes-and-you're-out-policy is one reason why wildlife officers in Colorado say it's so important to try and find a way to coexist with bears. We, as humans, can actually protect them and prevent them from being destroyed if we act responsibly and don't attract them to our homes to begin with.

It's becoming a difficult situation. Across the nation, more and more people are moving into what was once bear country. More people are also playing in bear country. This means that, inevitably, there will be more human-bear encounters. In Colorado, in particular, this is definitely the case. Wildlife officers are also finding that they're running out of places to relocate the bears. They feel that the most strategic way to battle this problem is to try and educate the public about how to live with these large predators.

Black bears are the most common of all the bears in North America. They're agile creatures, able to run as fast as 35 miles per hour. They can climb trees and they're also strong swimmers. When the land was less populated by humans, bears primarily dwelled in forests, and open space in mountainous areas, feeding on wild berries, acorns, plants, insects, and occasionally meat from other animals, particularly carrion. Now, developments have broken up those large expanses of uninhabited lands, forcing bears to find food where they can.

In the winter, bears hibernate as a way of surviving during a time when it's difficult to find food. During the warmer months they're active—mating, breeding, hunting, and feeding. This is the time when it's most likely that we'll come in contact with them.

The forests are still a large part of bear country. However, bear country now includes some of our suburban areas, especially those that are in the foothills or wooded areas. Our homes are often helpful to bears because our trash, pet foods, bird feeders, barbecue grills, and other things provide them with food. If bears find food in a particular area or at a particular house, they'll frequent that area or house to keep feeding themselves. This behavior puts us in a position of having to adapt to living in bear country.

Bears will eat almost anything. They'll eat anything we eat, as well as your pet's food, hummingbird food, bird seed, and even livestock food. The biggest thing you can do to prevent bears from coming around, as well as to protect them from eventually being destroyed if they become a nuisance, is to take away that food source.

Don't leave your trash outside. If you do, get a bear-proof trash can. You can contact your local division of wildlife for information on where to get one. It helps as well to clean your trash cans regularly with hot water and bleach to kill off some of the odors that attract bears to begin with.

Try to feed your pets inside, and don't store their food outside. If you have to store some pet food outdoors, make sure that it's also in a bear-proof container. Bring in hummingbird feeders and other bird feeders at night. Bears can be active at any time of the day or night, but they're most active during the early morning and dusk. Generally they rest during the day.

You can also discourage bears from coming around by cleaning your barbecue grills to get rid of any grease. You may even want to store your grills in the garage or a storage shed. Compost piles and ripe garden vegetables or fruits can also attract bears. If you have beehives, they can also be a problem. Contact your local division wildlife for help with fencing designed to keep bears out.

Bears are just one of several predators that you may encounter. Others include mountain lions, coyotes, bobcats, lynxes, wolves, and foxes.

Mountain lions are one of North America's largest wild cats. They can weigh as much as 275 pounds.

These predators may be looking for food in our neighborhoods as well. Mountain lions are one of North America's largest wild cats. They're very powerful animals, able to bring down deer and elk. A adult male weighs an average of 150 pounds and can be about eight feet long. They're easily identifiable by their size, long tails, and tawny color.

Lions are generally found in areas where there are healthy populations of deer, their main prey. These creatures are elusive, roaming in territories that can be well over 300 square miles. If they don't have deer to eat in their remote, primitive territories, they may follow deer into our suburban areas in order to feed themselves. They may feed on smaller mammals, livestock, or domestic animals.

Lions generally stalk and kill their own prey. A powerful bite below the base of the skull will often break their prey's neck. Lions will drag the carcass to a sheltered spot beneath a tree or some sort of overhang and feed on that carcass for a few days.

Again, we heighten our chances of coming in contact with lions when we move into mountain subdivisions, or when their main prey, deer, frequent our subdivisions. One way to keep lions from frequenting your own home is to not attract deer or other mammals to your property. You may want to refer to the chapter on wildlife-proofing your home for help on how to do this. Also, keep your pets from roaming free. They're easy prey and they may attract lions. Try to bring your pets in at night. If you have to leave them outdoors, make sure they're in a secure pen or one with an electric fence. Secure your livestock in sheds or barns at night and keep the doors closed. Bring baby animals in close during baby season.

Larger pastures that contain young cows and sheep can be protected by fences between six and eight feet tall or electric fences. Guard dogs and donkeys can also be helpful. Unfortunately, the conflict between ranchers and predators is one that's ongoing without much solution. Contact your local division of wildlife or your state extension agency for suggestions on how to prevent predator attacks on livestock.

This advice is good for all of the predators. Generally, they're elusive and shy. Most don't want a confrontation and will do anything they can to avoid one. However, situations like starvation can cause them to become more brave. They may come around humans more than they would have before, searching for food. They may either be following other wild animals like deer or rabbits that are also coming around our subdivisions for easy food, or they may be searching for domestic animals or trash if they can't find enough of their regular prey.

The more often these predators come around, the more accustomed they'll become to humans. This could be a bad situation for both the animal and us. It's more likely that we'll have a confrontation in this case. Someone could get hurt and the animal could be destroyed. Wild animals, no matter how tame they appear, are always wild and unpredictable.

An incident in the San Isabel National Forest in Colorado turned out badly for both a boy and a black bear.

A 16-year-old boy was camping with some family members in the forest. According to a report by the Colorado Division of Wildlife, the bear went to the campsite early in the morning and bit the boy on the shoulder as he slept. Despite several scrapes and puncture wounds, the boy chased off the bear with a shovel, but it wasn't enough to scare the bear away. The DOW says the bear came back a second and third time, chasing the boy's father onto the top of his pickup truck. The father then shot the bear twice and killed him.

Wildlife officers say one of the reasons the bear may have been so aggressive is because food was sparse that summer. They say a late June freeze damaged acorn-producing oak brush, as well as other plants that bears like to eat. Hence, the plants didn't provide food in the late summer as they usually do. This forced many bears to have to look for food elsewhere. That reason, coupled with the fact that bears are attracted to campsites for food, is what may have caused that bear in particular to be so aggressive. Also, if that bear was a regular at campsites, he may not have had much fear of humans. He may have been accustomed to seeing people, perhaps even realizing that he could rely on them for food.

Playing in bear country, or any other predator's country for that matter, is much different from dealing with these animals on our own turf. When you're out in the wilderness, there are some things you should do to try and protect yourself.

Camping is one situation where you may be likely to encounter a predator, primarily a bear. Bears are very attracted to campgrounds because of the food they provide. If they've been fed by humans before, they may not be as shy as they would normally be, and they'll begin to associate humans with food. This could mean a bear might be aggressive and pushy if he thinks you have what he needs.

The most important thing you can do is keep your campsite very clean. If the campground provides bear-proof trash cans, be sure to take all of your garbage to them instead of leaving it lying around your campsite. If you don't have a place to empty your garbage, bag it, or even double bag it, in plastic bags and store it away from your tent. Don't try to burn or bury your garbage because bears can still find scents and will try to dig it up out of the ground or your firepit.

Store your food safely! Keep all of your food and coolers in your car trunk, or suspend them from a tree. The recommendation is that you suspend food at least 10 feet off the ground and four feet from the trunk of the tree. This will help keep bears from getting to it. Be sure not to store your food in the same place where you sleep. This could be a dangerous situation for you! If you have food smells on your clothes from cooking, store those away from your tent in a secure place.

If you have been cooking, be sure to thoroughly clean your barbecue grill or stove. Any leftover bits of food or grease will attract bears or other wild animals. If you're using a table, wipe it clean. You may want to bring a grease-cutting cleaner with you to make sure all of the residue and smells are gone.

Toiletries, especially perfume, may also attract bears. Bears tend to be attracted to sweet smells and will try to get at those as well. Store those away from your tent or sleeping area. Make sure they're in a secure place. You can protect yourself while you sleep by making sure that you're practicing good personal hygiene.

If you store your toiletries, food, or smelly clothes in your car, lock it. Bears are more clever than you might think! Colorado wildlife officers had to deal with a situation in southern Colorado where a bear was breaking into cars! The bear wasn't breaking the windows, either. He had actually learned how to open a certain type of car door. He would do just that and search the cars for food. When food is the motivating factor, wild animals can learn a great number of tricks!

If you're not camping in predator country, you may be hiking in it. There are some good tips you can follow to protect yourself against predators.

Try to avoid hiking at dusk and dawn. These are active times for bears, in particular, and avoiding those times will decrease your chances of bumping into one.

It's a good idea to make as much noise as possible while hiking to give animals a chance to realize that you're coming. You're more likely to be attacked if you surprise a wild animal. Make as much noise as you can while you hike. You can carry a walking stick to tap the ground, or even singing will give animals notice.

Avoid walking in heavily wooded or brushy areas. You can't see as far in areas like this and you never know when you may round a bush and bump into a bear or a mountain lion. Try to stay in open areas where you can see what's going on around you.

If you're hiking with small children or pets, it's best to keep them with you at all times, or at least make sure they're in your sight. You should have your dogs on a leash, not only for their safety, but also because some states have laws against dogs running free and harassing wildlife. Whenever possible, try to hike in groups or with another person. This always helps to make the situation seem more threatening to a wild animal, meaning that animal will be more apt to avoid you than confront you. It's also good because you'll have help if someone were to be hurt.

You're most likely to get attacked if you surprise a predator like a bear or a lion, or if you come too close to one who is feeding, or to a mother with young. If you do come across any of these situations, immediately move away. If the mother has young, be sure to give her a way to escape with her babies. Just as you would try to protect your kids against someone who was threatening them, a wild animal will also try to protect her young if she feels that you're a threat. Wild animals have no way of knowing what your intentions are and they're scared. Generally they'll try to avoid conflicts with you and find a way to escape. Don't linger to try and entice the babies to pet them or take pictures of them.

Whether a bear or a lion has young or not, try to stay calm if you come across one of them in the wild. Stop or back away slowly, but whatever you do, don't run. This can trigger a natural instinct in a predator to chase you. You will not be able to outrun them. Don't climb a tree to escape a bear; he could follow you. Keep facing the animal as you back away, backing up in a direction that will give the animal a way to escape and avoid you.

The mountain lions I worked with at the sanctuary really provided me with a clear window into mountain lion behavior. Whenever I started down the path to the grassy alley that ran between several large enclosures of mountain lions, they would crouch down and hide as I walked by. They thought that I didn't see them. Although these lions were typically ex-pets, exhibiting more playful behavior, it was a fine line between play and hunting for prey. The lions would wait until I was a few feet away, and then they'd pounce or charge toward the fence at me. If I ever ran alongside the fence, they would run too, chasing me with wide eyes as if I were a deer. Their natural instinct is to hunt, and running away from them is a good way to become hunted.

If you're confronted by a mountain lion, talk loudly and firmly to try and intimate him. Back away slowly, giving the animal a way to escape. Do what you can to try to appear larger than you are. Pull your jacket or sweatshirt up above your head. If you have a small child with you, put your child up on your shoulders. This will make you look larger and protect your child in case he or she may panic and try to run. Generally lions will take down old, sick, or young prey before they attempt to tackle healthy prey. If your behavior is animated and if you look large, you may not be a lion's first choice.

If the lion starts to come towards you, throw stones or branches—whatever you can—to try and frighten him away. Try not to crouch down or turn your back to the cat. Wave your arms and continue to speak loudly and firmly. All of this will help to convince the lion that you're a threat. If you're attacked, do whatever you can to fight back. Try to remain standing, fighting upright.

If you've been confronted by a bear, talk aloud to him. He may stand upright or move closer to you to try and smell you. Once he realizes what you are, he may leave. A bear's eyesight is good and his sense of smell is keen. The bear may try to intimidate you by charging you and retreating. Keep backing away slowly. If the bear does attack, fight back with whatever you can. Bears have been driven away by people fighting them with rocks, sticks, or whatever they have on them as well as their bare hands. Pepper spray is something you can carry with you for self-defense.

A male mountain lion gives a fair warning not to come any closer by hissing.

Coyotes are a pretty common sight but they're generally elusive. Attacks on humans are extremely rare, although there have been cases where they have attacked small children. Coyotes are more likely to lose their fear of humans in urban areas as they become accustomed to us. Up close and personal confrontations with bobcats or lynxes are practically non-existent.

Bears and lions are the two major predators you have to be very aware of while hiking in their country. Lions in particular, however, are rare to see in the wild, as are instances of them attacking humans.

To put this into perspective, here are a few statistics from Kevin Hansen's book: *Cougar, The American Lion*.

Hansen refers to a study by Paul Beier that found that "from 1890 to 1990, there were 53 recorded cougar attacks in the United States and Canada." From these attacks, some of which involved more than one person, 10 people died and 48 were injured. Hansen tells us, for comparison's sake, that deer-car collisions were responsible for 130 human fatalities in 1989 alone, and that "each year in the United States, domestic dogs kill 18 to 20 people and inflict 200,000 injuries" (69).

As a member of the media, I feel that when we do hear about a predator attacking a human, we tend to amplify it because of its rarity. While we don't even report every death from a car accident, stabbing, or shooting, a death or even an injury by the teeth and claws of a predator is very rare. In a time when we battle more with traffic, technology, and predators in the corporate world, fighting for your life against a wild animal is a return to our raw and primitive condition. It's not as common as other types of trauma, so when it does happen, it seems to get more attention.

Seeing past the fascination may help to put it all into perspective. There was a time when we, as humans, knew what we needed to know to protect ourselves against predators, and live with them as best as we could. Today, all we're doing is learning that we need to gain back some of that education about wildlife that used to be a part of our schooling just to stay alive. There was a time when our two worlds were intertwined. They separated for awhile in some circles on this planet, but the time has come when we're being forced to learn how to live more closely together again. We are recognizing once more, this is a world in which we have to live together.

Here's a summary of this chapter's advice:

- secure all trash
- keep compost piles covered
- pick ripe vegetables and fruits immediately
- bring in pet food and water
- bring in hummingbird feeders and bird feeders at night
- bring in pets at night
- keep barbecue grills clean
- install electric fencing
- secure young livestock at night
- buy a guard dog or donkey
- don't attract other animals like deer that may be prey

Avoiding Predator Confrontation:

- make noise when hiking
- avoid heavily wooded areas with limited visibility
- keep pets and children with you
- don't approach wild animals with young
- face the animal
- back away slowly
- talk loudly
- put jacket up over head to appear larger
- put child on shoulders to appear larger
- throw sticks and fight if attacked
- carry pepper spray
- don't run

7

Ducklings in My Swimming Pool

There are about 150 species of ducks, swans, and geese world-wide, an approximate third of which live in North America. These species have webbed feet, and most of them are aquatic, meaning they'll take to the water for food, shelter, and to raise a family. When you think of water habitats, you're probably thinking of ponds, lakes, and calm rivers. But what if that water habitat happens to be your swimming pool?

If you have a pool, you may find that it's being used by many creatures aside from those in your family! I remember a call from a distressed family who discovered about a dozen ducklings in their pool one day. The family kept their pool uncovered, leaving an open invitation of water for wild ducks. Sure enough, a family of them decided to take advantage of that invitation.

It seemed harmless enough. The ducklings were swimming around and appeared to be enjoying themselves. What this family didn't know, however, is that a joyful day at the pool could turn deadly for this duck family if they didn't take the proper steps to make sure those ducklings had a way out of the pool!

The little ducks were too small to hop out of the water onto the edge of the pool. This is the case for many baby ducks: the edge is too high for them and they're stuck. I told the family to put a board halfway into the water, creating a little ramp that the ducks could use to exit the water. Providing this little escape route saved the ducklings' lives. Again, they lacked the flight feathers necessary to take flight from the water as many species of waterfowl are able to do.

The family watched as the young ducks used the ramp to get to dry ground. However, the little guys walked out of one problem and right into another. Now, they were in a fenced-in yard and the parents were on the other side of the fence. The family figured that the ducklings had wandered through a small crack in the fence in order to get into their yard. Now, they were a bit disoriented and unsure how to get out.

I told the family to herd up the ducklings and put them in a deep cardboard box. Once they did that, I instructed them to take the box of ducklings to the other side of the fence and let the parents take over once again. They tipped the box on its side and left the area immediately so that the parents wouldn't feel threatened and could resume care of their babies. The parents flew down from the tree where they had been watching this entire scenario unfold, and led the babies away.

Pools can be dangerous for ducklings like these. Often, they can't hop back out once they've hopped in!

Muscovy ducks, like this one at the Wildlife Rescue sanctuary, are a common sight in parts of Texas. They often hang out near water in suburban areas.

Often, ducks jump into pools to enjoy the water. However, the little ones that haven't developed wings and can't fly have no way of getting back out of some pools once they're in them. When this is the case, you need to try to find some way to help them out. You can try what the family above tried. You can also try other things like a light bamboo mat that would float on the water, giving the ducklings something to stand on. You can use a straw broom with a long handle, securing it on the edge so it won't float away, giving the ducklings something to walk out on. You can also try overflowing your pool. The situation is yours to be creative with.

It may be surprising to you to know that ducks are quite common in urban and suburban areas. They'll wander through residential neighborhoods, down streets, and unfortunately, even down the medians of our highways. When there are a couple of parents leading a string of ducklings through these types of areas, there isn't much that we can do. These always appear to be scary situations for the ducklings, and they often cause us to panic. Our first instincts generally are to want to help them out of such dangerous areas. The fact of the matter is that some species of ducks, just like many other species of wildlife, have become urbanized. They choose the areas where we live for their own homes, and they seem to prefer city life over a more rural one.

When you see a family traveling through your neighborhood, one of the best things you can do to help them is to let them go on their way. Bring your pets indoors for awhile. Try to encourage your neighbors to do the same. Bringing in all pets, as well as children, will help keep the area quiet. This will help to keep the ducks calm and it will help them to keep going in the direction they were headed.

If there's traffic coming down your street and the ducks are trying to cross, flag oncoming cars to slow down so that the ducks can get to where they need to go. Help them to go in the same direction they're headed. If you try to chase them back the other way, they'll most likely keep trying to cross the street and then they could get injured. Take precautions not to endanger yourself as you do this. If you notice a family of ducks walking down the middle of the highway and it appears that they need to cross it, call the police for help. A situation like this can be a potential traffic hazard for drivers, especially since those ducklings are going to turn heads as people are driving down the highway, most likely going faster than 55 miles per hour. Police can help to slow cars down and lessen the likelihood of a serious traffic accident, as well as aid the ducks in crossing the busy highway.

Sometimes, these traveling families of ducks don't always stay together. As they try to make their way through neighborhoods, it's pretty common for a baby or two to become separated from the mother or parent ducks. If a baby has fallen into a hole, window well, or a ditch, help him out. All you have to do is scoop him up and point him in the direction of his family. If the family is too far away for the baby to see, gather him up and take him closer. The parent duck should hear the baby and resume care.

If all of the babies have become separated from the parents, gather them up and release them no more than 30 feet away in an area where the parents can continue to care for them. For example, if the babies are separated from their parents by a fence, gather them up and release them on the other side of the fence. You can also try to herd the babies toward a small hole in the fence where they may have entered.

If the babies have fallen down into a storm drain or a window well and you can't reach them, use a long board to help them out. Position the board so it acts as a ramp, giving the babies a way to walk out. Regardless of what you do to help the babies, don't worry about your human scent scaring the parent ducks off. This won't affect a reunion.

If you're afraid that an entire family of ducks is trapped in an unsafe area like a maze of neighborhood yards with dogs, contact a rehabilitation center for assistance. Again, if you don't know how to get in touch with wildlife rehabilitators in your area, contact your local state wildlife agency to get a list of people. It's often impossible to relocate an entire family of ducks safely and effectively. You can abandon the ducklings if you try to catch them and take them to another area by themselves. It's quite difficult to catch perfectly healthy parent ducks who can fly. The only solution may be to let the ducks go on their way. It's also important to remember that when we think of ducks, we often picture them in a serene, wilderness setting. Many of these duck families we're talking about in this chapter are urban ducks, well accustomed to the things we perceive as dangerous. Many of the ducks know what to do and how to get out of difficult situations when given the chance.

The youngsters are often the ones who get into trouble when they're left behind or abandoned. If you've discovered an abandoned baby you will have to get him to a wildlife rehabilitation center. First of all, make sure the baby is truly abandoned. Leave the area and watch for about a half hour to see if any parent duck comes back to reclaim the baby. If you can't find the parents or the rest of the family, gather the baby up and put him in a cardboard box with some tissue on the bottom. This will give him something to grip onto. Make sure you put the baby in a deep box. Ducklings can jump quite high, and tree ducks have claws on their feet that enable them to climb.

It's important to get the duckling to a rehabilitation center because wild ducks are very hard to raise in captivity. They need around-the-clock care, the proper diet, and the proper environment to keep them alive and well. It's also good for their social skills if they're raised in an environment with other ducklings. The biggest reason to get help is that most wild ducks are federally protected. It's illegal to keep them and raise them without the proper permits.

While you have the duckling, put a heating pad halfway under the box to provide warmth. Put a towel between the heating pad and the box. Be sure it's not under the entire box, so the duckling has a way to escape the heat if he's too hot. If you have to keep the duckling for several hours, position a lightbulb so it's shining in one half of the box. Make sure it's not too close to catch anything on fire or get the duckling too hot. The lightbulb will provide warmth that the little guy will need.

Don't put any dishes of water in with the duckling. He could drown in even a little bit of water if he's weak. All it would take is for him to lose his balance, fall into the water, and be too weak to get out. You can pour a thin layer of water into something like the lid of a margarine container. Don't keep the little guy in water either for any period of time. Again, ducks can drown if they have no way to get out of the water. You can feed the duckling a temporary filler of puppy chow soaked in water to fluff it up. Once the little guy arrives at a rehabilitation center, he'll be raised on a proper diet especially for waterfowl. A proper diet and socialization with other ducks is crucial to him having a second chance at life in his natural environment.

It's always a great delight to watch these little ducklings grow up and return to a life in the wild. They seem to pick up right where they were left off. The fact that many of them have that second chance is because of people lending a caring hand and allowing a kind heart to guide them.

Here is a summary of this chapter's advice:

- put floating ramps in pool so ducklings in water can get out
- reunite any ducklings with parents by putting them near parents
- bring pets and children indoors during reunions
- cautiously slow traffic in your neighborhood when ducklings cross road
- call for police when ducklings are causing a traffic hazard on highway
- remember not all ducks live near water

8

Thumper, Flower, Meeko, and Who Knows What Else?

We all wondered who had the family of raccoons living at their place. A new mother had made her first summer appearance with her six youngsters, bringing them out with her on her nightly rounds for food. Most of the neighbors were involved because their houses were regular stops for this raccoon. The question we all had as neighbors, however, was, whose house she had turned into her own. After all, this family of seven had to be holed up somewhere!

It didn't take long to figure out where she raised her new family. One of my neighbors caught her in the act of moving her young one night at dusk. He was sitting on his back porch enjoying the last bits of sunlight from a wonderful summer day when he saw the mother raccoon emerge from his neighbor's chimney. She paused at the top and then returned to the darkness to retrieve something—one of her babies.

He didn't know why she was moving her young. It seemed like a vulnerable situation for the babies. After all, where was she moving them to? Would they be all right in the meantime? Apparently, there was no need for worries. My neighbor watched as the mother went to and from the chimney, carrying one baby away at a time. She repeated the process until each of her six babies had been moved to a new location. We never knew if that homeowner knew he had raccoons in his chimney. Whatever the situation, the mother made up her mind that the chimney had served them long enough.

After the move, we still saw the mother and her babies on a nightly basis. We didn't know where they were living but we knew that they were all right. We watched them become stronger and stronger as the days passed, growing into teenage balls of fluff that were as playful and ornery as any raccoons could be. It was tempting to want to intervene during that seemingly vulnerable time, but we later saw that mom knew what she was doing all along.

It's difficult to know when the right time is to intervene, if a baby animal does need your help. Most of the time, baby animals are all right. Their parent or parents are usually somewhere nearby, taking care of them as they should be cared for. This chapter attempts to explore the behaviors of some common animals that people encounter. Hopefully, it will give you the guidance you need when you feel doubt about a situation involving a baby animal.

One animal that's commonly misunderstood, and commonly mistaken for a rat, is the Virginia opossum. Only, this animal isn't a rat, but rather a marsupial, and a beneficial one for that matter! A marsupial is a mammal that usually has a pouch on the belly. This is where the females carry their developing young. The Virginia opossum is the only marsupial in North America north of Mexico.

Opossums eat insects, snakes, small rodents, and carrion. They also like berries, fruit, and some vegetables. Opossums have been known to kill and eat rattlesnakes, minimally affected by the rattlesnake's bite. If you're afraid of snakes you might not mind having the opossum as a neighbor!

The opossum is a gray or blackish furry creature with bare feet, ears, and tail. The female gives birth to anywhere from one to 14 embryonic young about the size of a dime. They then make their way from the base of the mother's tail up into her pouch where they attach themselves to her nipples within. They only emerge when they're old enough to come out and ride on their mother's back or

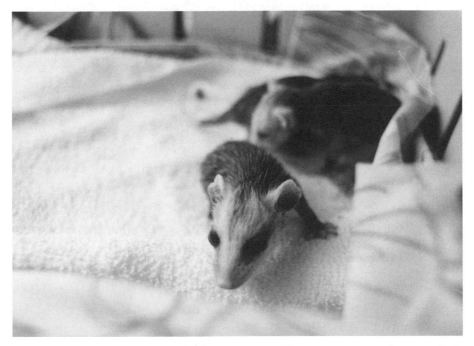

These young opossums were abandoned. Too young to survive on their own, they were taken to a rehabilitation center for help.

follow her around. This is usually after about two months. Opossums can stay with their mothers for up to six months.

As the young opossums grow, they'll get too big to ride on their mother's back all at once. It can get a little crowded up there. Imagine around a dozen babies on her back! If she's startled and takes off suddenly, a baby or two can get left behind. The mother doesn't keep count of her babies. If they're too young to keep up, they may be abandoned. This may be the time when you'll find one.

Sometimes, the babies are old enough to survive on their own, so getting left behind won't affect them much. A good rule of thumb to try and determine whether or not a baby is old enough to live on his own in the wild is to measure the length of his body. A opossum who is about six to eight inches long, not including the length of his tail, is capable of taking care of himself. Babies that are smaller than this should be taken to a rehabilitation center where they can get some help. If the opossum is six to eight inches long, but obviously injured in some way, or unusually thin with his ribs showing, he needs help as well.

The best way to gather up a young opossum is to put on a pair of gloves and throw something like a towel or a t-shirt over him. Opossums have sharp teeth and can bite, but generally they'll do whatever they can to get away from you. They may act one of two ways. Sometimes, they'll become so scared that they'll slip into a catatonic-like state and hardly move at all—hence the term "playing opossum." They may even roll onto their sides and shut their eyes. Opossums may also try to scare you by opening their mouths and showing all of their 50 teeth, hissing, or screeching. This is often their way of bluffing. The best way to gather up a opossum, no matter how he's acting, is to tip a cardboard box in its side and use something else, like a shovel, to gently push him into the box. You can also use a pet carrier to contain the animal.

Once you have the opossum in the box, shut the lid and make sure that it's taped shut so the opossum doesn't escape. Make sure that there are air holes in the box so that it doesn't become too stuffy in there. Leave the t-shirt in the box with the animal to give him something to grip onto or hide in. As is the case with all wild animals, opossums will be the calmest if you keep them in a dark, quiet environment. Try to keep them away from noise, activity, and pets to help reduce their stress level.

There's one other situation in which people commonly find abandoned opossums. This is when the mother gets hit by a car. Even if the mother is killed, the embryonic young inside her pouch may still be alive. Often, these young can be saved, but it's important to get them to a rehabilitation center right away.

Cover the entire opossum with a towel, and again, tip a cardboard box on its side and use something else to push the mother into the box. You should be able to tell if the mother has young because her pouch may be moving. If the young are old enough, they may still be around the mother or on her back. If this is the case, check the area for young that may have wandered away from their mother. Follow the above procedure to gather them up as well. If you're on the side of the roadway, be sure you're considering your own safety. If you're with someone else, have that person look out for oncoming traffic. You never want to get so wrapped up in saving an animal that you endanger your own life.

Once at the rehabilitation center, the baby opossums can get the critical care that they need. If the mother is injured, she can also get help. A rehabilitation center can provide the opossums with the proper formula that they need to grow healthy. They'll also be raised with other opossums, giving them the opportunity to socialize with their own kind. This will help them immensely when they're released back into the wild.

Opossums can easily become completely dependent on humans for food and care. Three huge opossums came to the sanctuary one day who knew nothing about fending for themselves or the wild. They didn't even know what kind of food they were supposed to be eating!

A couple had raised these opossums from tiny babies that barely fit in the palms of their hands. By the time they were full grown and came to us at the sanctuary, they each weighed about 20 pounds. This couple had fed them everything that they ate. They ate Twinkies, table scraps; they even drank Big Red soda. These opossums were dependent on this couple. They even licked their faces, recognizing them as their providers in life.

The couple brought the opossums to us because they had decided that they needed to be in the wild. The couple didn't want to just dump them in the wilderness after having raised them in a household. They brought them to us, hoping that we could help integrate them back into nature where they should be.

This was a very difficult task. At the sanctuary, we fed all of the animals natural foods, foods that they'd be eating if they were in the wild fending for themselves. These foods were usually supplemented with cat and dog food, a good form of nutrition for many species of wildlife. We didn't have Twinkies or Big Red soda to feed the opossums. Instead, we fed them fruits, vegetables, even carrion or birds that had passed away.

The problem was that these opossums weren't used to eating those other foods. Not only were they not used to eating natural foods, but they didn't even like them! For awhile, they refused to eat. All three of them lost some weight before they finally started eating what we put in front of them. Once they were eating and on a stable diet, the next step was to get them used to being outside.

We started by putting them outside in secure enclosures for small periods of time. Those periods of time became longer, until finally, they lived outside. They adjusted well to the Texas heat. It didn't take long after that before the opossums started to act like opossums again. They soon began taking a fancy to fruits and vegetables, as well foods they would come across and eat in the wild.

The three fat opossum pets that once wouldn't drink anything but Big Red soda nor eat much more than Twinkies were soon trim, healthy, and ready to go. They were taken to private land in the Texas hill country where they were let go to continue living out their lives where they belonged.

Even though the opossums weren't raised on very healthy food, at least the people tried to take care of them and eventually brought them to the sanctuary. Opossums are hearty animals and take quite a bit of disturbance in their lives. One animal that's particularly sensitive to stress and handling, however, is a wild rabbit. Hares, like jack rabbits, are also very sensitive.

Cottontail rabbits are perhaps one of the most common types of wild rabbit that people encounter. People find baby cottontails all the time. The female will generally build her nest on the ground. This means it's more likely you'll stumble across it. The nests are shallow depressions, usually lined with the female's fur and dry vegetation. Often they'll look for a place in brush or tall grasses. Some females build their nests under sidewalks or under places like dog kennels. A female can have anywhere from three to eight babies.

These nests may turn up in your yard. We'd receive several calls from people who had accidentally run over a nest full of baby rabbits while mowing their lawn. Often, they're hard to see because the female will cover her babies with layers of soft fur from her breast, as well as dry grasses or leaves. When the babies are hit by a lawnmower, they're almost always injured and sometimes killed. Most of the time, they'll need help.

If this happens to you and one of the babies has a serious injury, it's very important to get him to a wildlife rehabilitator right away where the baby can be raised in a very secluded environment. Raising wild rabbits is a very difficult job, and it usually doesn't end well when someone tries to raise one on their own. These rabbits tend to have a high death rate when raised in captivity. In the wild, rabbits are hunted by several different species of animals. They generally have to be more alert while they're out fending for themselves. Bringing one of these little guys in from the wild makes them extremely nervous and scared. They see you as a predator. Those feelings of fright alone can kill them.

The only reasons a baby rabbit should be raised in captivity is if he has an injury that's so serious that it prevents him from getting around. The other reason is if a baby is truly abandoned. If you've run over a nest full of cottontails and the injuries are serious, get the babies to a rehabilitation center. If the babies have only minor nicks but still can hop around, leave them in the area for the mother to continue to care for them. They have a much better chance of healing themselves in the wild than in captivity. If you've accidentally disturbed a nest but the babies are all right, keep the nest where it is but tidy it up a bit. Replace any of the brush or fur inside the nest and cover it well with dry grass.

The other situation which warrants bringing babies into captivity is if the mother has been killed and the babies are abandoned. However, you must pay close attention to make sure that the mother truly has abandoned her babies. Female cottontails will often feed their babies only in the early morning and at dusk. If you're watching the nest, it's easy to think that the mother is gone for good. However, it's important to watch through the duration of the day, especially at dawn and dusk, to truly see if the mother is coming and going.

If you want to be certain that the mother is still around, what you can do is sprinkle some flour or some baby powder around the nest. Check the area later for tracks. If you find them, that usually means the mother is coming and going. You can also put a few strands of long grass across the top of the nest. When the mother comes to care for her young, she'll usually move the grass. This is another good indication that the young are being cared for.

If you're certain the mother is dead—perhaps you've found her dead nearby—get the babies to a rehabilitation center. The only exception would be if the babies are large enough to fend for themselves. Cottontail rabbits mature quite quickly and are capable of being on their own at a young age. If the baby has all of his fur, his eyes are open, and he fills the palm of your hand, he's capable of being out on his own. You may even notice him eating bits of grass or grazing. This is a good sign that he's independent. You don't need to take young rabbits to a rehabilitation center if this is the case.

This same rule applies to jack rabbits. However, these hares are independent at an even earlier age. They're born fully-furred with their eyes open. They'll leave the area where they were born as soon as a day afterwards, beginning to hop around and eat small bits of grass within a week. The mother will return about once a day to feed them until they're weaned a few weeks later.

If you have abandoned babies who don't have their eyes open, who don't have much fur, and if they're smaller than the palm of your hand, take them to a rehabilitator. Rehabilitators usually have good techniques for raising young rabbits in environments where they won't be as stressed. They also have milk formulas that are specific to wild rabbits. This will ensure the babies will grow on nutritionally balanced food.

To transport a rabbit, put him in a dark cardboard box with air holes. You can also use a pet carrier. If you use a carrier, put a towel over the door so he can't see what's going on around him. Try to put something in the box or carrier like an old t-shirt or a towel so the rabbit doesn't slip around as much. Try to keep him in a dark, quiet environment to keep his stress level down. Keep pets away from the box as they could greatly stress him. You can put some green grass in the box to give the bunny some familiar scents, or food if he's able to eat.

If you've noticed a rabbit nest in your yard and you're just curious about the babies, there's no harm in just leaving them there to grow up right in front of you. If you have pets, you should try to keep them out of the area until the babies have hopped from the nest and have gone off on their own. This generally takes a couple of weeks. Dogs and cats commonly catch or even kill baby bunnies so their best chances of survival are without any in the area.

Watch the babies grow up from a distance. If you interact with the nest too much, you could scare the mother away. If you've accidentally touched the nest or stumbled across the babies, however, don't worry about your human scent scaring the mother away. Human scent doesn't usually cause abandonment.

Often, situations involving wild baby animals just need a little help from humans. I remember once hearing scratching noises coming from one of the window wells in our basement. I pulled back the curtains to discover six baby skunks had fallen down into the three-foot-deep well. The mother was peering down on her babies, not sure what to do to get them out.

The solution was quite simple. My dad and I put a board down into the window well. It acted as a plank. With the mother calling her babies from above, they were encouraged to try and reach her. Once they realized that they could use this plank to get to her, they were out in a matter of minutes.

The first baby took a cautious step onto the wood, unsure of himself. As his mother's calls continued, he finally began to crawl upwards until he had reached his mom. Once that baby went, the others followed, one by one with their little tails sticking straight up in the air. The reunion was complete! Once the family went off into the night to forage for food, we put a chicken wire screen across the top of the window well to keep the babies from falling in again.

Skunks are another common species you'll find in suburban areas. People stumble across babies all the time, sometimes even during the day. While adult skunks generally aren't seen out during the day, young skunks sometimes are. Their nocturnal behavior seems to settle in a bit later in their development.

If you see a baby skunk out during the day, it doesn't necessarily mean that the little one needs help or is sick. A young skunk will often go out and wander about, learning his own way of life. He may look young and vulnerable but generally he's OK. Skunks are usually eating on their own and quite independent by the time they're anywhere from six to eight inches in length, not including the length of their tail. They'll often wander about, learning how to forage for food and exploring the environment.

If you find a young skunk doing this, it's best just to leave him alone. Trying to approach the baby can startle him, causing him either to run into a dangerous situation like a roadway, or to become disoriented or lost. Sometimes young skunks won't run from you at all. They're not born with an instinct to be afraid of humans. That develops over time. It's best to leave the skunk alone to go on his way. Usually his mother is somewhere nearby and he'll venture back to her. If the little skunk is staggering or falling over, obviously sick or injured, call a wildlife rehabilitator for advice on what to do. A skunk that is lying motionless on the ground is in need of immediate help.

It's best that you let a professional handle an injured or sick skunk. Skunks are one species that can contract rabies and it's a good precaution to let someone who's trained to handle wildlife deal with the situation. If you're bitten, you'll most likely have to get rabies shots as a precaution. Also, the skunk will have to be killed and tested for rabies as well. It's a risk that's not worth taking. You can discuss the situation with the wildlife rehabilitator you're in contact with.

Skunks are generally born in den-type environments. A female will seek out natural shelters like hollow fallen logs, or use large rocks with den-like crevices as places to have her young. Skunks also use den-like areas under sheds, garages, and houses for their homes. The females can have anywhere from four to seven young, although this will vary depending on the species. Generally, the mother will venture out of the den at night to search for food. When the babies are old enough to follow, they'll go with her.

If you come across a skunk den and aren't certain whether or not the mother is caring for the babies, you can sprinkle baby powder or flour around the entrance to the den and check for footprints later. You can also monitor the den at nightfall to see if the mother is coming or going. While the mother is nursing, it's common for her to leave her babies for hours at a time. As long as you see her coming and going, you'll know she's caring for her young.

If you know the mother has been killed and has left behind a den of babies, contact a wildlife rehabilitation center for help. Wildlife rehabilitators have special milk formulas designed specifically for the species they're trying to raise. This will ensure the baby skunks get the proper nutrition. The rehabilitators also raise the young animals with others of their own kind so that they're properly socialized. This will help them interact with their own species when they are eventually returned to the wild.

Another animal that prefers to build homes in den-type environments is the raccoon, popularly identified by a black face mask outlined in white. This is another species that lives with us in our suburbs and even in our cities. In the wild, raccoons use places like tree hollows and rock crevices in the woods, wetlands, and along wooded streams to raise their young. However, in our neighborhoods, they'll use crevices under sheds, houses, chimneys, attics, abandoned buildings, wood or brush piles, or hay stacks for homes. The females prefer to have shelters that will protect them from the wind, rain, and other elements.

Raccoons can have anywhere from one to eight babies. Those babies generally remain in the den where they were born for up to eight weeks. After that, they'll begin to follow their mother on nightly excursions, learning how to forage for food. As the raccoons get older, they'll begin to venture out on their own a little bit at a time. By the time they're about four months old, they'll be ready to start lives of their own without their mother and siblings.

If you're concerned about the young raccoons, unsure whether or not they're being taken care of, you can use the above-mentioned technique to put your worries at ease. Raccoons are most active at night, so you can start by watching the den at night to see if the mother is coming and going. Be sure you watch from a distance so you don't scare the mother. You can also sprinkle baby powder or flour in front of the den and check for footprints later. You can also lightly secure a piece of cardboard in front of the den. As the mother comes or goes, she'll move the cardboard to get into the den. If you don't have any confirmation that the mother is coming or going, and if you can hear chattering or crying from within the den, the babies may be abandoned. Often, abandoned babies will wander from the den, crying for help. In either case, contact a wildlife rehabilitator for help.

There are times when you'll see raccoons out during the day. This is sometimes the case with a raccoon that may be particularly hungry, and it's sometimes the case with teenage raccoons. As with skunks, nocturnal behavior isn't usually developed until the animals are older. You may also see breeding raccoons and mothers caring for young out during the day.

At Wildlife Rescue and Rehabilitation, I would often observe teenage raccoons fumbling around in the oak trees out behind the house. They were exploring their surroundings, learning how to climb and play. They would often climb down the trees onto the back porch to eat cat food. Sometimes, they would just sleep in the trees during the day. This isn't an unusual sight, and there's no need to be alarmed if you see a raccoon behaving like this. If you have raccoons sleeping in your trees, just leave them be until nightfall. They're not stuck. They're accomplished climbers and they have no problem going up and down trees. Nightfall is when they'll come down and begin feeding. If you have pets, keep them out of the area at that time. Barking dogs can scare and keep raccoons up in trees all night!

A raccoon who's wandering around during the day, crying out or stumbling, may be abandoned or in need of help. This is especially true if he's extremely thin, emaciated, or lying on the ground unable to walk. It could be that he's been abandoned and has gone without food for several days. If this is the case, contact a wildlife rehabilitation center for help. It's better to get assistance from a professional in this case. As with skunks, raccoons can contract rabies. Due to this, if you are bitten, you'll most likely have to get rabies shots and the raccoon will have to be destroyed so that he can be tested for rabies.

You never know what type of encounter you may have when it comes to baby animals. A Texas couple found themselves chosen as the caretakers for fox kits one night.

The couple told me their story over the wildlife hotline. They said they watched one night as a mother fox brought her babies, one by one, up onto their porch. They had seen the fox around on a regular basis and didn't think much of it. However, when the mother fox began putting her babies in an empty pet carrier on their porch, they began to get suspicious. It was at that point that they noticed the mother fox didn't seem like herself. She seemed lethargic or sick. She wasn't acting as healthy as she normally did.

Once all of the young foxes were in the pet carrier, the mother turned and left. The couple didn't see her return that night, or the next. They decided to go out and check the area for her. They found her dead. The couple called the wildlife hotline, knowing they had to get the babies some help. They were sure at that point that the mother fox had deliberately left her babies with them, hoping that they would help them. That's the interpretation this couple gathered from the situation so they brought her babies to our sanctuary.

There's no telling what killed the fox in this story. Foxes can contract rabies as well as distemper, a viral disease. Both of those can kill them. The situation above is something anyone could experience. Foxes live amongst us and have learned to adapt to our man-made environment. In wilderness areas, foxes try to raise their young in dens. Those dens can be along the banks of streams, in rock piles, and in hollow trees and logs. In suburban America, foxes can use man-made places that simulate a den they might find in the wild. A female fox will have anywhere from one to 10 babies, depending on the species of fox. They're known to be very shy and nervous. They're primarily active at night, but they're also out and about around dawn and dusk.

It's also common to see foxes in trees. The common gray fox is a wonderful climber and will often take shelter in trees, or just hang out in them. This species generally prefers to rest in trees that are thick and provide good cover. If you see a fox in a nearby tree, there's no need to be alarmed. Again, the fox will come down at nightfall to go and hunt for food. If you have dogs, keep them out of the area because they can keep a fox treed all night long!

If a baby squirrel falls from his nest and it's too high for you to reach, you can put him in a cardboard box with bedding, or some other sort of make-shift nest, and secure that in the same tree.

An animal you can expect to see living in the trees is a squirrel. Many species of squirrels make their nests in the trees with leaves, bark, and twigs. Just as baby birds fall from the nest before it's time for them to start venturing out with mom, squirrels do the same thing. If you find a baby squirrel on the ground, separated from the rest of his family, you can return him to the nest. If the nest is too high for you to reach, you can put in him a cardboard box with tissue or bedding on the bottom and secure that in the tree as close as possible to the nest. The mother squirrel should continue to care for the baby. If the baby has been severely injured, he should go to a rehabilitation center.

In reading all of this information on baby animals, you may realize that they all have something in common. Although they may appear frail and helpless, most of the time they're not. Many of them are independent at young ages, or relying on a parent who's somewhere nearby. Generally, a wild animal's best chance of survival is in the wild. No matter what kind of wild baby you stumble across, keep the above advice in mind. It generally applies to any species. Give a parent adequate time to return and care for his or her young. Observe carefully. That behavior may bring you the answers you're looking for!

Here is a summary of this chapter's advice:

- observe for hours to see if there's parental interaction
- observe at night
- put flour in front of den to see if parent is coming and going
- secure cardboard at den to see if parent is coming and going
- watch from a distance
- keep pets and children out of the area
- keep the area dark
- remember that wandering and crying young may need help
- take young with serious injuries to a rehabilitation center
- remember that it's sometimes normal to see young out during the day, alone

9

If You Hate Mosquitoes, You'll Learn to Love Bats

The schoolteacher was desperate for information on bats. She needed to find out all she could in a hurry. Only, she didn't want the information to help her teach kids about these furry, flying mammals. She wanted the information so she could help save some lives.

Earlier that day, four bats were trapped inside the school where she worked. When school administrators and security personnel found out, they became frantic. Unfortunately, there are many myths associated with bats that cause people to panic. People often think that bats will suck your blood, become tangled in your hair, and dive bomb you to try and attack you. They also often believe that *all* bats have rabies. Those are just myths, and they may have been some of the exact myths in the minds of administrators when they ordered that the bats be killed!

A custodian was elected to "take care" of the bats. All the administrators were sure that these bats were a serious health threat to the students. They told the custodian to get rid of them however he felt fit. That custodian used a can of Raid insect killer and sprayed the bats.

Two of the four creatures died from the deadly poison within minutes. The other two managed to cling to life. They were trying to fly and get away, but the poison was slowly overcoming them. They were soon grounded, or unable to take flight any longer. They could only flap their wings slowly on the floor of the school.

This is about the time that the schoolteacher stepped in to save the bats. At this point, they were obviously no threat to anyone because they were so sick. She took pity on them and decided to get them to a place that could help them: Wildlife Rescue and Rehabilitation, Inc.

The teacher put the bats in a cardboard box and called the sanctuary for help. We had a network of drop-off sites within the city of San Antonio—anything from veterinary clinics to people's own homes. We directed her to the site closest to her. From there, one of the sanctuary's many volunteers drove by, collected all of the animals destined for Wildlife Rescue, and drove them to us.

I could smell the Raid before the volunteer walked through the door of the main house. He was carrying several boxes full of injured and sick animals. Right away, I could tell which boxes contained the bats. The stench was enough to make me sick. When I opened up the box, one of the two bats had already died. The last one was still fighting for his life.

We treated this strong and courageous little brown bat. We cleaned him up, removing all of the Raid from his body. We also gave him fluids to help wash the poison out of his system. We kept a close eye on the little guy, constantly encouraging him to take more fluid to regain both nutrition and strength.

Within just a couple of days, the bat had become stronger. His senses were sharp, his strength was back, and he was able to fly. We decided not to hold him back any longer than we had to. He had proved he had the energy to make it back out in the wild where he belonged. I took him outside one night to let him do just that: return to the wild. Holding him in the palm of my gloved hand, I help him up to the trunk of a tree. Immediately he reached out and gripped it with his elongated fingers at the ends of his wingtips. Quickly, he climbed up and away from me. Once he was high enough to drop into flight, he lifted his face to the night's breeze as if studying the wind to decide which direction he would go. The decision was fast— he leapt from the tree. I watched his erratic flight path until he was gone.

This little bat's story is reason enough to try and dispel some of the common myths about bats. One of those myths has many people believing that bats suck blood. That's not entirely true. In North America, most all of the species of bats are insectivores, meaning they feed on insects only. Others feed on plants, going after the nectar, pollen, or fruit. There is a species of bat that feeds on blood: vampire bats. They'll make a small incision with their teeth, usually on livestock, and lap up blood. However, the vampire bat doesn't live in North America.

The bats that live here are amazingly beneficial. According to Bat Conservation International in Austin, Texas, a single brown bat can consume about 600 mosquitoes in just one hour. The 20 million Mexican free-tailed bats that live in Bracken Cave, Texas, eat 250 tons of insects each night. Bats are an incredible means of insect control.

Another common myth is that bats will purposely fly near you and become entangled in your hair. Again, this is just a myth. Often, bats do fly close to animals to eat insects that may be swarming around them. They also have a naturally erratic flight pattern. It's full of dips and dives that can easily be mistaken as dive-bombing. Bats use something called echolocation to fly. This is similar to a radar or a sonar system. They emit a series of sound waves which bounce off any objects that are in the vicinity. These sound waves are then reflected back to the bat, letting him know how big and how far away things are. This system helps bats both to avoid bumping into things and to zero in on prey like insects. If you listen carefully while outside on a warm night, especially in an area where there are quite a few bugs, you can hear these chirps and clicks.

Bats can contract rabies, as can many other different types of mammals, but that doesn't mean that all of them are carrying the virus around. Rabies is a virus that attacks the central nervous system. The brain and spinal cord become inflamed. When an animal has rabies, he loses control of his muscles and becomes very unco-ordinated. The animal will usually stop eating and drinking. Some victims of rabies appear very lethargic when they have it, but others become very aggressive and can attack anything around them. This is because rabies can manifest itself in one of two ways. The aggressive pattern is a sign of "furious rabies"; the lethargic pattern indi-

A single bat, like this big brown bat, can eat his body weight in insects every night. Photo by Merlin D. Tuttle, Bat Conservation International.

cates "dumb rabies." When an animal begins to show symptoms of rabies, he will usually die within a few days.

A precaution that you can take to prevent getting rabies is to have any pets, like dogs or cats, vaccinated for the virus at your local veterinary office. Teach your children that they shouldn't handle bats, as well as any other wild animal. Teach them that they shouldn't go near a bat that's on the ground. If you or anyone else is bitten by a bat, you should report it immediately to your doctor or your local health department. The bat should be tested for rabies. If the bat tests positive you will have to undergo post-exposure rabies vaccinations. Those vaccinations are no longer as painful as they used to be, and they're given in the arm instead of the stomach as they used to be. The only exception to getting the vaccinations is if the bat tests negative for the virus. According to Bat Conservation International, there is about one human death a year from bat rabies. To keep things in perspective, however, the organization reports that dogs attack and kill more humans each year than bat rabies, and that bats are not a high-ranking threat to our lives.

When a rabid bat is found, it's often a big story on the local television stations, as well as the front page story in the local newspapers. However, one bat, as well as statistics, can easily get blown out of proportion. For example, in Colorado, the percentage of bats testing positive for rabies averages 15.2 percent according to the Colorado Division of Wildlife. However, this percentage is based on bats that people found and brought in for testing. Some of these bats are already sick, making them easier for people to catch and submit for testing. This percentage of infected bats is not an accurate percentage for the entire bat population in Colorado. The Colorado Division of Wildlife estimates that less than one percent of all bats in the state may be infected with rabies.

Keeping this information in mind, it may be easier to deal with conflicts involving bats—like having one trapped in your home or business.

The solution can be simple. Keep calm. Remember that although the flight pattern appears unstable, bats are very good navigators and won't run into you. Try to get the bat outside by turning off the lights and opening a window or a door. If you open your window, be sure to open your screen. People often forget to do this because they're panicking! When this is done, the bat should detect the open window or door and fly outside. If a light is on outside, the bat may naturally be attracted to it because he knows that where there's light at night, there are insects! Give the bat some time to leave.

Bats are nocturnal, or active at night. If you discover that one is trapped indoors and it's day time, it may be hard to get the bat to leave. It's also dangerous for a bat to fly during the day. I recall a couple of instances where bats were shooed out the door during the day. Almost as soon as they took off outside, large birds swooped down and ate them.

I remember walking across my college campus in Montreal, Canada, when I heard a bat frantically squeaking. Unless you've heard a bat squeak or chirp, it's difficult to recognize the sound. I knew the sound from researching bats, and I knew that one was somewhere around me, in trouble. It didn't take me long to find him. A raven had the bat in his mouth and was trying to eat him. The raven was standing on the grass, picking the bat up and putting him down, trying to reposition him for eating. I took a step toward the bird and he flew away. I approached the bat. He was lying on his back, wings fully outstretched, panting. He was in such shock, it was easy to gather him up. I took off my flannel shirt and wrapped him in it. I brought him home and put him in a dark cardboard box until nightfall.

Once night arrived, I put on my leather gloves, gently gathered the bat up, and took him outside. By then, he was recovered from his stress. He was angry, snapping his teeth at me. He was anxious to go. I held him up against a tree where he grabbed hold and instantly dropped into flight. Flying at night gave him a much better chance of survival without any ravens around!

If you have a bat who's trapped inside your house or business and you can't wait until nightfall for his release, you can still take him outside. Take a broom and gently push the tip of it against the bat's body. He should step onto the broom. Once he's there, take him outside and gently place him up against a tree trunk or a tall bush. The bat should climb to the highest point and wait there until nightfall. Once it gets dark, the bat will take off to feed. If you're uncomfortable with this, call a wildlife officer or a local rehabilitator for help.

You can also escort a bat outside by catching him under a coffee can or some other type of container. When the bat has landed and is still, carefully place the container over him and then gently slide a piece of cardboard underneath the container. Be very careful not to crush the bat's delicate wings. Be sure you wear thick gloves for protection. Once the bat is under the coffee can and the cardboard is in place, take him outside and place him up against a tree or large bush. Remove the container. Again, the bat should climb to the highest point and wait until nightfall to take flight.

The reason why it's so important to offer the bat a tree or a large bush is because it's very difficult for a bat to take flight off the ground. Many species of bats can't do this, and they need to find something tall enough to crawl up, at which point they have enough height to drop into flight. A healthy bat may occasionally get grounded, but if there's something around to crawl up, he will.

There are some situations, however, where a bat is injured or sick and will be unable to do this. If a bat is lying motionless on the ground on his back or stomach, he probably needs help. If this is the case, the bat will generally make no effort to move. In this situation, call you local wildlife agency or a rehabilitator for help. It's best you don't handle the bat at all. In fact, some states prohibit handling of bats. You can put a cardboard box over the bat while you're waiting for help. This will protect him from predators and extreme weather until someone comes to get him.

Some species of bats will become grounded when they have too many young. Most bats have one to two babies, but the eastern red bat, for example, can have three to four. There isn't strong evidence to indicate that these bats carry around their babies in flight, but the young often do attach themselves to the mother. When this happens, she can become weighted down. If something scares these bats or if they're knocked out of their tree for some reason, they'll stay on the ground because they're too heavy with young to take off. People often do find these bats in this situation.

If this is the case, you generally don't need to worry that these bats are sick. They're just stuck. You can help the bat out by gently pushing a broom up against her body. Then, take her to a nearby tree and let her climb onto the trunk. This will help her protect herself and keep away from predators. Once in the tree, the mother may take flight. She may also just need some time to rest before going out to feed again. If the mother bat repeatedly winds up on the ground, contact a rehabilitation center for assistance. She may need help.

If you find that the mother bat flies away but leaves behind one of her babies, that baby may need to get to a rehabilitation center as well. If the baby is on the ground, gently use a broom and try to get him to step onto it. Take him to a nearby tree and see if he's able to grip onto it and climb. If the baby is old enough to fly, he'll do so. If he's unable to fly, call a rehabilitation center for help. You may want to watch the young bat throughout the day and into nightfall. Once it's night, he may take off. If he still hasn't at that point, he needs help.

Many people complain of bats roosting in their home or business. Bats are capable of squeezing through openings that are smaller than an inch in diameter. Bats particularly like to roost in attics and in chimneys. Solitary bats will generally live in the cover of leaves in trees. However, social bats tend to seek out caves, the hollows of trees, and protected places in buildings and houses where they can cluster together in colonies. These bats will spend quite a bit of time resting or roosting. Bats are active at night, so they generally rest during the day.

There are two parts to dealing with roosting bats: exclusion and prevention. Exclusion involves humanely repelling the bats from their location. Prevention is making sure that they don't come back and roost in your place any time again in the future.

Watch at dusk to see exactly where the bats are leaving from. You can then exclude them by making a one-way door. This way, the bats can exit their roosting site but not return. Lightweight bird netting is a very effective one-way door. Cut a piece of netting and hang it over the opening where the bats are leaving each evening, securing it with either a staple gun, tacks, or duct tape. Make sure the netting is a couple of inches from the opening so that the bats are able to leave without getting entangled. Drape the netting a couple of feet below the edge of the opening. This will allow the bats to leave, but they will be unable to get back into their roost when they return.

It's very important not to use this exclusion technique while the bats may have young inside that are unable to fly. If the young can't be cared for by the adult bats, they will starve to death. This is unnecessary death for these bats, not to mention the fact that it will leave a very smelly mess on your hands after they die. It may cost you more in the long run to try and remove all of the corpses than it would have if you just waited until the young were old enough to fly.

To determine if there are any youngsters being left behind, check the roost after dark when the adult bats have left to feed. According to Bat Conservation International, most bats have young in the United States in June and July. You may want to wait until several months after this time period to begin excluding the bats. At this point, the youngsters will be self-sufficient and able to go out at night and feed just like the adults. Also, most species of bats will leave in the winter time, migrating great distances south where they continue to remain active. This would also be a good time to apply your exclusion techniques. If you have any questions about when to repel the bats, you can give Bat Conservation International a call.

When you are excluding bats, give them at least a week to leave their roosting site and find new places to rest. This should be enough time to make sure that all of the bats are out. Once that time has passed, check the area with a flashlight to make sure that they're all gone. When they are, that's the best time to apply your prevention techniques.

Start by carefully inspecting the entire perimeter of your home or business. Be sure that all doors have draft guards beneath them. Seal any other areas around other doors. Weather strip, as well as seal and plug any small openings that you can find, replacing loose and rotting boards. It's also a good idea to cap your chimney. Make sure that there are no places where bats can get into the structure through any of your walls, roof, or eaves.

If you enjoy the benefits of bats and would like to have them around, just not living in your house, you may want to check into bat houses. These are wooden boxes that can be mounted on poles or tree trunks, usually 12 to 15 feet off the ground. The opening for the bats is in the bottom of the box. They should be in places that are protected from harsh weather elements, and they should face east where they'll get sun in the morning but shade in the afternoon. Bats also seem to like these houses when they're near water sources like rivers, lakes, bogs, or marshy areas where there may be more insects.

These homes are appealing to bats and they'll often use them as roosting sites. They're good ways to keep these beneficial creatures nearby without having to share your own home with them! You can find exact designs for bat houses by contacting Bat Conservation International.

Here is a summary of this chapter's advice:

- make sure there are no young in the roosting site
- wait until young are grown and can fly to seal site
- turn on bright light at night in roosting site
- use ammonia to help repel bats
- create a one-way door with netting outside an entrance/ exit
- wait a week until all bats are gone from roosting site
- apply weather-strip
- seal all holes and fix loose boards

10

There's a Snake Asleep in Our Jeep

We all have trouble getting to work every once in awhile. Perhaps the car won't start, or perhaps you'll have a flat tire. Perhaps you'll even have a snake asleep in your jeep!

It may sound crazy but it happens more than you might think! A woman called our wildlife hotline, frantic. She told me she couldn't go to work because there was a snake under the hood of her car, curled up right next to her engine. She had no idea what to do.

We told the woman to put a line of flour or baby powder around her car so that we could keep track of the snake. If he was to leave without anyone seeing, the woman would still think he was in her car. By placing a line of powder around the car, we would be able to tell if the snake had slithered off at any point because he would leave a track.

The next step was to try and get the snake to leave her car. Snakes generally crawl up under the hood of cars because they like the warmth from the engine. Snakes are cold-blooded, meaning their body temperatures are the same as their surroundings. The warmer the environment, the more active they are. Underneath a hood is also a quiet, dark hiding place. Often, the midday sun is too hot for a snake. They like to keep warm, but they don't like to bake in the sun during the hottest time of the day. Engines can be ideal resting places.

In order to get the snake to leave, we would have to try and make the environment uncomfortable for the animal. We would have to alter the environment so that it was just the opposite of warm, quiet, and dark. We first took away the "quiet" by turning a radio on near the engine. This made it noisy and uncomfortable for the snake. Then, the woman opened her hood so that the hiding place would no longer be dark. Lastly, I told her to lightly sprinkle the snake with water from her garden hose. Luckily she had one nearby. She turned it on and lightly sprayed the snake. The cool water make him uncomfortable and he immediately left the area. The woman then went on her way to work, with quite the excuse for being late!

You may one day find a snake under the hood of your car. As I told the woman, one of the most effective ways to get a snake to leave is to sprinkle him with water. The combination of noise, light, and water is the most effective, however. If you don't have access to a garden hose, you can always use bottled water and squirt that on the snake. You should not try to scare the snake away by starting your engine. This could injure or kill the snake if he becomes caught in a moving engine part. That would leave parts of him all over your car and you would be stuck cleaning up the mess.

Snakes don't cause panic in people just when they curl up next to their car engines. They can also cause panic if they're living around people's homes. Snakes have always made some people feel uncomfortable. People often strike out in fear and kill the snakes. They kill snakes even if they're not poisonous or posing a threat.

Many of the snakes you'll find in your garden or around your home are harmless. There are poisonous snakes to watch out for, however. The best way to identify a snake is to go to a bookstore and pick up a field guide that will help you identify snakes and reptiles. What you thought may be a poisonous species may turn out to be harmless. For example, rat snakes can have skin patterns similar to some species of rattlesnakes. They'll even vibrate their tail, making a sound similar to a rattle.

You can identify venomous snakes, like this timber rattlesnake, a member of the pit viper family, by looking in a reptile field guide. Photo by Kip Ladage.

Another example of easily mistaken species involves the scarlet kingsnake and the red milk snake. These snakes have color patterns similar to the venomous western coral snake. Both have colorful rings that are red, yellow, and black. The way to identify a coral snake, however, is to look and see if the red and the yellow rings are touching. With scarlet kingsnakes, as well as red milk snakes, the red and yellow colors are separated from each other by a black ring. There's a famous mnemonic rhyme that goes something like this: "Red and yellow will kill a fellow; red on black, friend of Jack." Even though western coral snakes are venomous—they're relatives of the Indian cobra—the snakes are so small that it's nearly impossible for them to open their mouths wide enough to bite you. The circumference of their bodies is usually not much greater than that of your pinkie finger.

No matter whether a snake is venomous, any one of the species can be helpful to you. They're carnivorous predators that eat

Most species of snakes, like this garter snake, are harmless and beneficial. Photo by Kip Ladage.

various small animals like rats, mice, frogs, fish, insects, earthworms, lizards, and even other snakes. If you're having a problem with rodents or insects, one of the best things you can do is allow these snakes to live in your yard.

If this isn't something you can do, it may be easier than you thought to humanely repel the snakes. If you're noticing several snakes around your home, it could be that you have a rodent problem or an insect problem. That may be a result of leaving food scraps lying around, or too many nooks and crannies in and around your home that need to be sealed up. If you have a rodent problem you'll need to fix that first. Otherwise, you'll have snakes on a regular basis. As long as the food source is there, they'll keep coming around.

Next, take a look around your home to see what type of environment you might be offering these snakes. They like warm, dark places to hide. If your yard is full of rock piles, wood piles, or trash piles, you may be providing excellent homes for snakes. Tall weeds and low brush may also provide good homes for snakes. The first step to discourage snakes is to clean up all of these piles, taking away their places to hide. Keep any tall weeds or grasses cut low. This will also eliminate hiding places and discourage them from loitering in your yard.

Take a look at the foundation of your home. Loose boards that have rotted and fallen to the side will also provide places for snakes to hide. Be sure to carefully inspect the foundation of your home and seal up any nooks and crannies that could be good homes for snakes.

If you already have snakes living under your home, garage, shed, or porch, you can repel them the same way you would any other wild animal. Try to place a light in the dark area to make it unpleasant for the snake. You can also toss ammonia-soaked rags back into the area. Sprinkle cayenne pepper or naphthalene flakes in there as well. These smells should make it too uncomfortable for the snake, causing him and others to leave. Don't dump any of these products directly on the snake because this will just cause agony. There are also commercial snake repellents available. However, there are mixed reports on how effective these really are.

Use these repellents for about a week. Sprinkle baby powder in front of the entrance to the hiding place. This will give you a way to see if the snake is coming and going. If you don't see any tracks after a few days, the snake is most likely gone. At that point, seal up any holes and replace any loose boards, permanently sealing off the area. While you're doing this, you may want to put some metal flashing around the foundation of your home, extending it several inches below the ground. This will discourage any tunneling.

It's important to repel snakes during the summer months when they're most active. Snakes will remain dormant during the winter months, so you won't see them at that time, or much in the fall. Repelling during the summer will help you better monitor the situation to make sure the snakes are leaving. It will also give them a chance to find new shelter somewhere else before the colder months set in. You don't have to worry about young being left behind. The young are self-sufficient once they're born. Snakes are also fairly mobile so it shouldn't be too difficult for them to move on and find a new place to live.

Since snakes are fairly mobile, you may not have to do much to repel one that's in your yard. There's a chance that snake could just be passing through. A sighting doesn't necessarily mean that you have an entire nest of them living around your home.

If you want to monitor a specific area to see if snakes are coming and going on a regular basis, again, you can sprinkle flour or baby powder around the place you're monitoring. If you repeatedly see tracks, it may mean that the snake or snakes are living in the area.

If you don't discover a snake in your yard, you may discover one in your home. This is obviously a case of an unwelcome guest! Try not to panic; the snake wants to find a way out just as much as you want him out. Given a chance to escape, most snakes will take it.

Try to confine the snake to an area where there is a doorway. Open up the door and give the snake a chance to escape. If the snake is near the door, but not going out, use a broom to gently herd him toward the outside. You can also turn on a radio, or a bright light if it's nighttime, and try to encourage the snake to leave on his own.

He'll most likely head for the fresh air. If the snake is in a place like a bathroom, where there is no doorway to the outside, shut the door and put a towel underneath it. This will confine him to that area and prevent him from escaping and getting lost in your house. You can either call a wildlife expert for help, or try to get the snake outside yourself. Most wildlife agencies prefer that you have the snake confined to one area before they send out help. This saves time by preventing an exhaustive search.

If you feel comfortable trapping the snake yourself, you can try doing so with a tall trash can. Tip the trash can on its side. Use a broom to gently herd the snake into the trash can. Generally, a snake can strike at a distance that's half of his own body length. A regular broom will usually give you enough room to guide the snake into the trash can at a safe distance. Once the snake is inside the trash can, stand it up and put the lid on.

Smaller snakes won't be able to climb up the slippery sides of the trash can. Longer snakes won't be able to get out as long as you have the lid secure. You can secure it by taping it or tying it shut. Take the trash can to a wild habitat away from your home, take off the lid, and tip the trash can on its side again. The snake will leave on his own. You shouldn't need to handle the snake at all. If he's not leaving, tip the trash can up so he slides out. All you need to do then is retrieve your trash can and leave. If you don't mind the snakes—just as long as they're not in your house—you can turn them loose outside in your garden. Try not to release any snakes near major roadways. If they try to cross the road they'll most likely be hit and killed by a car.

If you have a snake in your house but you don't know where he is, sprinkle baby powder or flour lines across the entrances to each room. When the snake passes over the line, not only will he leave a track but he'll leave a trail for a short distance. This will help you determine which way he's going and where he might be hiding. Once the snake is in a specific room or area, you can shut a door to confine him, or you can use a tall trash can and try to get him out right away.

If you're uncomfortable with any of this, call your local division of wildlife or a rehabilitation center for assistance. If you've encountered a poisonous snake, do not handle him or approach him. Keep pets away from him as well. You can try opening a door and encouraging him to leave by playing a loud radio and shining a bright light near him. This may be a situation, however, where you should call for help from a professional.

Another common scenario involving snakes is finding them in swimming pools. Often, the snake is just trying to get a drink of water. Snakes can swim. However, if they're in a pool, they often can't get out. This means that they'll eventually tire and drown. You can place something like a plywood plank into the pool so that the snake can get out. You can use a broom to gently herd the snake toward the plank. Once the snake has climbed on shore, he should leave the area. If the snake is harmless (i.e. ringneck or crowned snakes commonly found in Florida) you can just pick him out of the pool and release him in your yard. Be sure to wear gloves, regardless. Even if a snake is harmless, he can bite out of fear. It's about the only defense a snake has against us!

If you've captured a snake on a rodent glue trap, you can release him in a wild habitat without having to handle him at all. Try not to leave the snake on the glueboard for very long. He needs food, water, and a quiet, non-stressful environment to survive. You can put the glueboard out in a remote area and pour vegetable oil on the board, coating the parts of the board where the snake's body is stuck. Don't use any other type of oil, especially motor oil. This is toxic to animals. Don't pour the oil into the snake's nostrils or eyes as he won't be able to breath or see clearly. The oil will eventually break down the glue. The snake should be able to free himself in an hour or so.

Most snakes will bring you no harm, and can be left to live in your yard to play their part in the ecosystem. It's important not to panic when you see snakes. Most of the time, they're not venomous. Again, even the venomous ones will go on their way when given a chance to do so. Harmless snakes should bring you no fear, even if you see them hanging out in the trees. Species like the corn snake and the green snake are good climbers. Again, if you have a problem with insects or rodents, snakes will do their part to combat that problem. The part you need to play is allowing them to do this.

Here is a summary of this chapter's advice:

- make sure you don't have a rodent problem
- don't leave food around that will attract rodents or snake prey
- clear all brush, trash, and rock piles
- keep weeds cut low
- store wood off ground
- seal all nooks and crannies in and around your home
- apply weather stripping
- bury hardware cloth around foundation of home
- apply metal flashing around base of home
- use commercial repellents
- spread naphthalene flakes
- spread cayenne pepper

11

Wildlife First Aid and Rescue

He said he was the biggest bird he'd ever seen, and he knew when he saw him wandering around the dry, Texas hill country that made up his backyard, that this bird was out of place.

This young man called the wildlife hotline as soon as he saw the bird. The tall gray creature was obviously injured. He had a broken wing. This was confirmed when the man tried to approach the bird and he couldn't fly away. With birds, not being able to fly is a major indication that something is wrong.

As I pulled into the driveway of the small ranch house, the owner ran toward me, yelling that the bird had just managed to crouch down and crawl under his house. There was an opening about a foot and a half high. The bird went in there.

I got out of my car and pulled out a small blanket from the back seat. I also put on a pair of leather gloves. These two tools would be for my protection as I tried to capture the bird. From the man's description of him, it sounded like he was a great blue heron.

Great blue herons stand about four feet tall. Their pointed beaks are six to eight inches long, powerful tools that they use to impale their prey. Herons eat things like fish, amphibians, and small rodents. But they also use their beaks to impale their enemies when they're threatened! I would have to be very protective of my eyes, as well as the rest of my body, when I approached this cornered bird.

The opening that led underneath the house was narrow, only about a foot and a half wide as well as tall. I proceeded to crawl through, using my elbows to pull my body along the ground. The young man went around to a similar opening on the other side of the house and crawled through. He said he'd try to cut the bird off if he decided to escape through that opening.

This had to be one of my most gruesome rescues. Dragging my body through the dirt with spiderwebs dangling above my head was giving me the creeps. Not to mention I was going to have to approach this bird in a very vulnerable position: face first and on my stomach!

Together, the man and I slowly made our way to the dark corner where the bird was hiding. I could see his silhouette against the bits of sunlight that broke through small cracks in the foundation. As I got closer, my fears were confirmed. This was a great blue heron, only he wasn't so great. He had compressed himself from his normal four feet of height to about a foot high to hide under this house.

As I got closer, all I could think about was how herons defend themselves. If he was to strike at my head, I would have to act fast to protect myself from that powerful beak. I managed to pull the blanket out in front of me, positioning it so I could throw it over his head as soon as I got a little bit closer.

I could see the heron had a broken wing. It hung limply by his side. The bird appeared to be emaciated, thinner than normal for his kind. That may have been the reason why he didn't put up much of a fight. I was able to toss the blanket over his head. He didn't try to spear me.

I placed one arm around the bird's body and wings and began to drag him back across the dirt toward the opening. Since the bird's face was covered and he couldn't see what was going on, he remained calm and didn't struggle.

When we got outside, I gently held the heron's great beak with one hand while holding onto his body with my other arm. This way, I could control the beak if the heron decided to strike at me. I gently placed the heron in a large cardboard box that I had brought along.

The young man kept his eyes on the bird. I could see that he was quite curious about him. Only moments ago, he was complaining that this was the biggest, ugliest bird he had ever seen. Now, he had no words and watched with a certain respect as I loaded him up, wishing us luck as I drove away toward the sanctuary.

If you haven't yet come across an injured wild animal, you probably will. They're continually hit by cars, wounded by dogs, and shot. There are many ways animals can get hurt. Some waterfowl become entangled in fishing wire; baby rabbits and snakes often get run over by lawnmowers. If you ever come across an injured animal, there are a few general guidelines you can follow to help him and get him to a wildlife rehabilitation center.

The best thing you can do for both yourself and the animal is to be prepared. Keep emergency numbers handy for animal emergency centers, the local branch of your state wildlife agency, and any local wildlife rehabilitators. Keep them in a place where you can access them in a crunch. Sometimes, we don't think clearly in emergency situations and it really helps to have those numbers already in a rolodex, cell phone, tucked away in your glovebox, or stuck to your refrigerator. Put them in a place where they're readily available.

When an emergency happens, people scramble for help. I remember taking countless calls about not only wildlife emergencies, but emergencies involving an injured dog or a cat. Animal emergency centers are usually open 24 hours, and some wildlife rehabilitation centers have 24-hour hotlines. You'll save yourself a great deal of stress by writing down those numbers.

If you're writing down those numbers, that's a big indication that you're the type of person who will stop for an injured animal. If that's the case, there are a few items you should keep in your car to help you in an emergency situation with an animal.

Keep old towels and blankets with you. These are probably some of the most important items. Injured animals are going to be extremely disoriented and scared. They most likely can't comprehend what

Twenty-four-hour animal emergency centers usually handle injured domestic animals like dogs and cats.

just happened to them and all they want to do is get away from the place where they're at. The pain will also make them very defensive.

Throwing a towel or a blanket over an injured animal will help to calm him down. That animal doesn't know that you're trying to help him. He'll be scared and when he sees you coming toward him he's either going to try to get away or become very aggressive. Covering his head will often cause him to sit still. Darkness calms most animals.

Another useful item is a pillowcase. This is good for catching and transporting smaller animals like snakes, or for slipping over the head of larger, frightened animals like a opossum or a deer.

Keep some old sheets in your car. These will come in handy when you're transporting the animal. You can cover the seats of your car to keep them clean, especially if you're transporting a deer! It's best to put sheets down and keep the animal in the car with you rather than put him in the trunk of the car. The exhaust fumes may seep into the trunk and make the animal sick. Trunks also tend to be too hot or too cold, which can add to the stress or dehydration of an injured animal.

Carry a plywood board with you to use as a stretcher, as well as some rope or old nylons. The stretcher can really help out an animal with a back injury because it will keep his spine straight as he's being transported to and from the car. The rope and nylons can be used to secure the animal to the stretcher.

To use a stretcher, you lay the animal on his side and secure him by gently tying a sheet, rope, nylons, or by fastening a belt. You can use duct tape, but if you do, put some type of material like a towel or an old t-shirt between the tape and the animal's fur. This way, the tape can be easily removed without tearing the animal's fur, or skin. You can also use the rope or nylons if you need to gently tie the legs of an injured animal like a deer. Nylons are preferable because they're extremely strong, yet the material is gentle enough so it won't cut into the animal's flesh.

Keep a sturdy cardboard box in the car to transport small and medium-sized animals. The box will provide a dark, quiet environment for the animal and keep him secure while you're driving him to a rehabilitation center. Keep some heavy-duty tape with you to tape the box shut. It's very important that you make sure the animal can't get out while you're driving.

There was a woman who, I believe, was very lucky in escaping a serious accident when a porcupine got loose in her car. She had picked up the injured animal and put him in a cardboard box, but apparently, it wasn't very secure. On the way out to the sanctuary, the porcupine got loose and actually stuck her with a few quills while she was driving. To make a long story short, the porcupine made it to the sanctuary and she made it to the emergency room to get the quills removed. It could have been much worse! Even a small animal like a bird can cause quite a distraction if he gets loose, and it only takes a split second to have an accident.

If you'd like more security, keep an animal carrier in your car. These are commonly used for dogs and cats. A carrier is a plastic container with a handle on top, plenty of air holes, and a metal-mesh door that clicks into place. An animal can't open the door once it's locked.

If you use a carrier, place a towel over the door to keep the animal from seeing out. If the animal can see what's going on, he may become frantic and start biting or scratching at the door, trying to get out. It's a good idea to throw a sheet over the entire carrier so the animal can't see out the air holes as well. Be sure to keep an old towel in the carrier so the animal has a soft surface to lie on. That will also keep him from sliding all over the place; that plastic can get quite slippery!

If you're using the carrier for a bird, keep a branch handy that you can secure inside the carrier. Birds naturally perch, and they're much more comfortable and less stressed if they have something to perch on rather than standing on the bottom of the carrier. Carriers are also much safer for animals like birds than bird cages. A bird can severely injure his beak and wings on the bars of a regular bird cage trying to get out.

A few additional items you might need for an animal rescue are a flashlight, a pair of gloves, and a broom. It's very likely you'll find an

It's best to keep a branch in your pet carrier to give birds, like this injured great horned owl, something to perch on.

injured animal at night and have to rescue him in the dark. Many species of animals are nocturnal, or more active at night, and those species will be at greater risk of getting hit by cars as they cross our roadways.

The gloves will protect you against scratches and bites, although you shouldn't handle any animal at all. That's where the broom comes in handy. You can use it to push the injured animal into your cardboard box or carrier. This will help reduce the risk of a scratch or bite.

It's important to use these tools. Do not handle the animal. There could be a risk of rabies infection from skunks, raccoons, bats, and foxes. Often when people are bitten by these animals, the animal must be euthanized so that his brain can be tested for rabies. That's the only way the test can be done, and you may also have to go through a series of inoculations. Take extra precautions around these animals and do not handle them at all. If you need help, call a wildlife professional to deal with the animal for you. Being careless isn't fair to you or the animal.

To complete your animal rescue unit, there are also a few first aid items you can keep with you. A scissors comes in handy in case you have to cut a bird free from fishing wire, for example. Hydrogen peroxide is good for flushing out maggots that may have hatched in the animal's open wound. Gatorade or Pedialyte can help with dehydration. Tea tree oil, a natural remedy, is a good topical anti-bacterial agent and will help cut down on infection. Hypericum spray can be used as a topical anesthetic for pain. You can pick up tea tree oil or hypericum spray at any store that sells homeopathic remedies.

These items should only be used for light first aid, however. Leave all of the serious medical work up to the licensed rehabilitation centers or a veterinarian. Trying to fix things could cause more harm than good.

People brought birds with broken wings into the sanctuary, only they had tried to tape up the wings themselves. One man used duct tape to try to mend a tiny sparrow's wing. It took us hours to cut away the tape, piece by piece, and remove it from the wing. Tearing off that heavy-duty duct tape would have pulled out all of the bird's feathers, and probably broken the wing in a different spot.

Don't try to fix up any type of mammal either. Wrapping a broken limb too tightly can cause swelling and aggravation. Also, an injured animal needs some time to calm down. Working with him too much so soon after his injury can cause extreme stress. This could even lead to death.

Now that you have your rescue unit intact, you need to learn how to put it all to good use and get the injured animal from the wild to a rehabilitation center where he can get some help.

If you find an injured animal, take a moment to observe his behavior. The animal will either be lethargic or hardly moving, or he may be frantic and desperately trying to get away. Taking time to observe his behavior will let you know how easy or difficult it may be to try to contain him.

Things aren't always as they seem, however. Sometimes, wild animals, like people, can be temporarily knocked out from an injury.

One man found an injured deer on the roadway. The deer was still breathing but he wasn't conscious. The man put him in his car without covering the deer's head or tying his legs. The deer woke up while he was driving and tried to escape. Luckily, the man was able to pull over and call the wildlife hotline for advice and additional help before he got in some kind of an accident.

You always want to calm the injured animal down and secure him in some way so he won't escape in your car and cause commotion. In order to do this, the first thing you should do when you approach an injured animal is cover his head with a sheet or a towel to calm him down. This is also a good way to help an animal that might just need a hand, rather than a ride. For example, deer often get stuck in fences. Covering the deer's head will calm him down while you help him get out of the fence.

Pet carriers are good for smaller to medium-sized animals like this common gray fox with head trauma. He remained in the carrier while being treated at a rehabilitation center.

Be sure to wear gloves when approaching any wild animal. Even though the animal may look lethargic or weak, he could strike out and bite at any time. Wild animals are unpredictable. Another precaution you can take is to wrap your legs or arms in towels to protect against bites.

Once you've thrown a towel, sheet, or blanket over the animal's head, keep the head covered the entire time. Once the animal has calmed down, lay a cardboard box on its side, or open a carrier door, and use something else like the broom to gently push him into the container. Cardboard boxes and carriers are good for small to medium-sized animals. Be sure that the animal fits in the container you're putting him in and that he's not cramped.

Every night at the wildlife sanctuary in San Antonio, we received an entire load of injured animals from a volunteer who collected them at specific drop-off points and then drove them out to us. I and other staff would go through each box, one by one, assessing the injuries and getting each animal to where he needed to be. At that point we could give each the proper care. Most of the time, the boxes were too big for the animals, except in one extraordinary case.

I opened a box about a foot and a half high. I was startled to find a great blue heron crammed in there. As soon as the box was opened he stretched upward until he stood at his normal height, which was about four feet. The bird seemed to be awfully relieved to be able to stretch his long, lanky legs again after having made the 30-minute journey out to the sanctuary! Use an appropriately sized box! Not only can it be very uncomfortable for the animal, but it could suffocate him as well.

After you get the animal into a cardboard box, secure the box by taping it shut, but be sure to put several air holes in the box. If you use a carrier, cover the carrier with a sheet so the animal can't see out. Be sure to put bedding in either container, but don't put any food or water in with the animal. An injured animal will have no interest in eating and the food will only make a mess. Water can be dangerous, even in small amounts, because if the weakened animal collapsed into the water dish, he could drown.

Obviously, a cardboard box or a carrier is going to be too small for a larger animal like a deer. This is where the stretcher and rope come in handy.

Deer must be handled differently because of their size and their disposition. Deer are easily stressed and they will frantically try to get away from you when you approach them. Immediately throwing a sheet or a towel over the deer's head will help to calm him down and cut back on unnecessary stress.

Be sure that the deer's head remains covered. Then, use rope or nylons to gently but securely tie the deer's legs so that he can't kick free or try to stand up. Don't tie the legs too tightly, however, because a deer could seriously damage a leg straining to get free. If the deer has a spinal injury, usually identifiable if he can't move his back legs at all, use the stretcher to transport him and secure him with a sheet. Otherwise, transport the deer propped up on his side in a natural position, similar to the position he'd take while lying down. Don't talk to the deer or blast your radio during the car ride. Again, these are unfamiliar sounds and could add to the deer's stress.

If it's going to be awhile before you reach the rehabilitation center, you can put some of your first aid items to use. If you have a dehydrated animal, it's all right to give him a little bit of water, Pedialyte, or Gatorade via an eye dropper or a baster. Make sure not to get any in his nose. Using a baster or an eye dropper will help you control the amount of liquid you're giving the animal. Administer only one drop at a time. This will help to make sure that the animal has swallowed the liquid before you give him another drop. If you don't have an eye dropper or a baster, you can also give the animal fluid using a jug of water and a towel. Wet the towel with water and squeeze it slowly, letting the fluid drip, drop by drop, into the animal's mouth.

Watch closely as you're administering fluid. Too much too quickly can cause the animal to choke or even drown. You can tell if the animal is aspirating because fluid will start coming out of his nose. If this happens, don't give him any more fluid. If the animal is severely injured and not wide awake to take the liquid from you, don't give him anything at all. It'll only do more harm than good.

The hydrogen peroxide in your first aid kit is good for surface wounds, especially those that have maggots in them. Gently pour a bit of the peroxide into the wound and let it flush it out. The hypericum spray or tea tree oil can be applied after the peroxide is done doing its job.

In your adventures as an animal rescuer, you may come across some particular types of animals that require special instructions for their rescue, or extra precautions. It's possible that you won't be able to handle some of these animals yourself and will need to call on wildlife rehabilitators or your local state wildlife agency for assistance.

Be careful around all types of herons. Again, they use their powerful pointed beaks to impale not only their prey, but their enemies. They will strike at you, often aiming at your eyes—a keen way to

It's important to be especially cautious around birds like this great egret with a broken wing. They can use their long pointed beaks as weapons.

Ducks and geese can sometimes get stuck in a thin layer of ice that forms while they're sleeping in water.

disable their predators when they feel threatened. Approach a bird like this with a thick blanket, held open with both hands and held up high. This way, you can throw it over the bird and cover his head before he can decide where to strike. I would recommend getting assistance for herons, especially great blue herons, or having a wildlife rehabilitator walk you through the rescue over the phone. It could be too dangerous to rescue an animal like this yourself. Some rehabilitation centers insist that only their staff do these rescues.

Other birds to be careful of are birds of prey, like hawks, owls, and eagles. They hunt and kill prey with their strong talons. Eagles, in particular, have a grip so strong it can easily damage the tendons in your hand should you get in their way. These birds will often flip on their backs to defend themselves, facing you with their open talons. Throwing a sheet or a towel over the bird will calm him down, but you must use something else to slide him into a cardboard box. Don't try to handle the bird or grab his feet.

In the winter months, there are special instructions for birds and waterfowl, which often get themselves into trouble in two ways.

The first way ducks and geese get into trouble is by freezing in ice. These waterfowl usually sleep on ponds or lakes. If they're sleeping in a thin layer of water, it can freeze by morning. Sometimes what happens is a wing or a leg freezes into the ice as well, trapping the bird.

If the water's not too deep and you can reach the bird, free him by breaking the ice all around him. If the bird flies away, he's probably fine. But if he's been stuck in the ice for too long, he may be suffering from frostbite and need immediate care, in which case you should get him to a rehabilitation center. If you've found an injured duck, transport him the same way you would any other injured animal, in a cardboard box or a carrier. Don't transport him in water. Again, a weak, injured, or sick animal can drown in even the smallest amount of water—even a duck!

Frostbite is the other way a bird will get himself into trouble in the winter, and not just from sleeping on ponds and lakes. Birds can get frostbite just from being out in the elements. When they have frostbite, they'll often become grounded, or confined to the ground, and not able to fly any longer. If you approach the bird and he doesn't fly away, get him into a box or a carrier and get him some help. Don't try to warm the bird up with hot water or a hair dryer. This could cause tissue damage.

In the warmer months, you may come across an injured reptile. There are special instructions and warnings for some of these animals as well.

If you come across an injured snake, try to identify the type of snake before you approach him. Some species of snakes look like venomous species, but really aren't. It would help you to have a reptile identification book with you at all times. The most common venomous snakes in North America are different types of rattlesnakes. Rattlesnakes will almost always be identifiable by the beads on the end of their tails and their elliptical eyes. Rattlesnakes are born with a rounded tip on the ends of their tails. This is the beginning of the rattle that will grow larger throughout their lives. Rattlesnakes also have a diamond pattern on their backs and many scales on their heads. A rattlesnake will generally coil up and rattle his tail when he's preparing to strike. Do not approach a snake that is doing this. Snakes can strike a distance that is about one-third to one-half the length of their bodies. To avoid being bitten, use something else to gently push the snake into an open pillow case or a large cardboard box. Be sure to tie the pillowcase shut with twine or rope, and tape the box to keep the snake from escaping. If the snake is venomous and you're not comfortable with the rescue, again, call for help. This may be the best way to go. Generally, snake bites happen as a result of someone trying to capture, kill, or handle a snake.

Another reptile to keep a close eye on is the snapping turtle. The name serves the species well because these turtles can break a finger or tear flesh with their bite! This is the only way the turtle has to defend himself; it's not an act of aggression. The snapping turtle has a large head, and his upper jaw is slightly curved. The shell is usually tan, brown, olive, or black. These turtles also have a long tail. The mouth is the only fast-moving part of the turtle, however. If you avoid it and use something other than your hand to push the turtle into a cardboard box, your rescue should be successful.

There are a few important things to note about turtles. First of all, don't pick them up by their tails. The tail is part of the spinal cord and you can cause a serious injury to a turtle by picking him up this way.

The second thing to note is that if you find pieces of a turtle's shell around him, pick them up and take them with you to the rehabilitation center. Often, shells can be patched back together with a special surgical glue used by veterinarians.

Lastly, many of the turtles on the road aren't injured; they're simply trying to cross the road. If you want to help, put on gloves, pick up the turtle, and place him on the other side of the road far away from traffic. Be sure to put him off the side of the road in the same direction he was heading. Turtles do have a sense of direction and if you place one back on the side of the road from where he just walked, it's very likely he will eventually try to cross the road again. The next time, he might not be so lucky and get hit and killed by a car.

It's also important to leave the turtle in the area where you found him. Don't try to pick him up and take him to a pond or lake. Turtles have a home territory. If you pick one up and move him, he may try to migrate back home and cross through dangerous territory. The turtle you found may also be a tortoise, meaning he's a land turtle and doesn't make his home near water like a turtle.

If you come across a large, injured predator like a mountain lion, bobcat, coyote, or a bear, it would be best to immediately call a rehabilitation center or your state wildlife agency for assistance. It's extremely difficult to transport an animal like this without the use of tranquilizers and large holding cages, not to mention the danger involved.

Your own life should come first no matter what you're trying to rescue. It's easy to get a big adrenaline rush and become caught up in trying to save an animal, but it's important to keep a clear head and think about your own safety every step of the way.

Large mammals like mountain lions should never be handled by you!

A veterinarian friend of mine is scarred for life after having seen a situation where a woman didn't think clearly or put her own safety first. She had stopped to help a dog on the side of the road. He stopped as well, but before he could help, the woman was hit and killed by a car.

Pull as far off the road as you can, and leave your hazard lights on to alert drivers that you've stopped. Be alert. Just because you're on the shoulder of the highway or a road doesn't mean that you're safe. If the animal is in the center of a busy road, call local police, sheriff's deputies, or the state or highway patrol for assistance.

The roadways aren't the only places that are dangerous for you. Your safety could also be in jeopardy if you're trying to rescue an animal either stuck or stranded out on an icy pond or lake. The ice can be thin, and many of these rescues require hovercrafts or other equipment designed to help trained rescuers stay safe, and alive. If you're unable to reach a stranded animal out in the middle of a lake or a pond, try to contact a local fire department for help as well as a rehabilitation center. Firefighters are usually trained to do water rescues.

It's a good idea to become familiar with your resources. Call up your local wildlife rehabilitators to see how they work. You can often get a list of licensed facilities from your local state wildlife agency. All rehabilitators operate a bit differently. Some would prefer you don't handle any type of wild animal at all and will send staff or volunteers out to do the rescue. Others will tell you how you need to handle the situation and walk you through the rescue, step by step.

Getting an injured animal to a rehabilitation center is the only way to go. These centers are licensed through the state, and often through the federal government as well. You have to have permits to possess wild animals. In some states, however, it's OK to pick up an injured animal as long as you're in contact with a licensed rehabilitator and you're in the process of getting the animal to the center.

If you're really interested in being around and helping out wildlife, ask a local rehabilitation center if they have volunteer opportunities. Most rehabilitation centers are non-profit organizations and they're in need of all kinds of help. They often welcome volunteers, giving you the opportunity to do anything from animal care like feeding babies, to office work and fundraising. You could even volunteer to be one of the people who do rescues on a regular basis! However, you don't have to do anything you're uncomfortable with. Most facilities offer all the training you will need to perform whichever duty you're interested in.

My experience as a staff member at Wildlife Rescue and Rehabilitation, Inc., in San Antonio, Texas, began as a volunteer opportunity. I moved to San Antonio in 1993. At the time, I had prior experience with animals and I wanted to find a place where I could volunteer and continue to be around them. I put in a volunteer application at Wildlife Rescue and it was accepted about a week later.

I was a volunteer for only two weeks before I was hired as a full-time staff member. During that two-week period, I rescued a hawk, a baby opossum, a bull snake, a rattlesnake, a roadrunner, and a handful of injured birds. It didn't take long for me to realize that I loved this work.

I eventually went on to become the sanctuary manager, teaching new volunteers who were just like me—eager to learn and to be around animals. There were endless opportunities for these volunteers. Some did nothing but collect dog and cat food and drive it out to the sanctuary. Some were actively involved in animal rescues, while others just came out to clean cages and feed babies. Some people volunteered their time and resources to build new outdoor enclosures for the animals. Others just focused on fundraising. Schools also welcome educational programs for the kids, and there's plenty of opportunity to teach about wildlife.

I never knew a person who wasn't touched by the wild animals he or she encountered. I never knew a person who wasn't changed permanently because of them.

Here's a checklist of items to keep on hand:

- emergency numbers
- flashlight

- leather gloves
- pillow case
- old towels
- old sheets
- box or pet carrier
- branches for bird perches
- broom
- plywood board
- duct tape
- rope
- nylons
- scissors
- hydrogen peroxide
- Pedialyte or Gatorade
- eye dropper or baster

Afterword

With the wild in their eyes,

It is they who must die,

And it's we who must measure the cost.

—David Mallett/John Denver
"Wrangell Mountain Song"

References and Resources

References:

Brown, Gary. *Outwitting Bears.* NY: The Lyons Press, 2001.

Hansen, Kevin. *Cougar: The American Lion.* Flagstaff, AZ: Northland Publishing, 1992.

National Audubon Society. *Field Guide to Mammals (North America).* NY: Alfred A. Knopf, 2000. www.randomhouse.com

National Audubon Society. *Field Guide to North American Birds (Western Region).* NY: Chanticleer Press, 1994.

Resources:

Alaska Department of Fish & Game
P.O. Box 25526
Juneau, AK 99802-5526
(907) 465-4100
www.state.ak.us/adfg/adfghome.htm

Alabama Department of Conservation & Natural Resources
64 North Union Street
Montgomery, AL 36130
(334) 242-3465
www.dcnr.state.al.us

American International Rattlesnake Museum
202 San Felipe NW, Suite A
Albuquerque, NM 87104-1426
(505) 242-6569
www.rattlesnakes.com

Archway Wildlife Rehabilitation, Inc.
P.O. Box 17956
Boulder, CO 80308
(303) 774-8347

Arizona Game & Fish Department
2221 West Greenway Road
Phoenix, AZ 85023-4399
(602) 942-3000
www.gf.state.az.us/welcome.html

Arkansas Game & Fish Commission
#2 Natural Resources Drive
Little Rock, AR 72205
(501) 223-6300
www.agfc.state.ar.us

The Association of Sanctuaries
331 Old Blanco Road
Kendalia, TX 78027
(830) 336-3000
www.taosanctuaries.org

Bat Conservation International
P.O. Box 162603
Austin, TX 78716
(512) 327-9721
(800) 538-BATS
www.batcon.org

Bird-X, Inc.
300 North Elizabeth Street
Chicago, IL 60607
(312) 226-2473
(800) 662-5021
www.bird-x.com

California Department of Fish & Game
1416 Ninth Street
Sacramento, CA 95814
(916) 445-0411
www.dfg.ca.gov

"Camouflage Gardening," Patti Simons
16 Tiburon Drive
Austin, TX 78738
(512) 261-5001

The Chintimini Wildlife Rehabilitation Center
P.O. Box 1433
Corvallis, OR 97339
(541) 745-5324
www.proaxis.com/~cwrc

Colorado Bat Society
2525 Arapahoe Ave., Suite E4
Boulder, CO 80302
www.coloradobats.org

Colorado Department of Public Health and Environment
Disease Control and Environmental Epidemiology Division
4300 Cherry Creek Drive South
Denver, CO 80246-1530
(303) 692-2035
www.cdphe.state.co.us

Colorado Division of Wildlife
6060 Broadway
Denver, CO 80216
(303) 297-1192
www.wildlife.state.co.us

Colorado State University Cooperative Extension
Colorado State University
1 Administration Building
Fort Collins, CO 80523-4040
(970) 491-6281
www.ext.colostate.edu

Connecticut Department of Environmental Protection
79 Elm Street
Hartford, CT 06106-5127
(860) 424-3000
www.dep.state.ct.us

Contech Electronics, Inc.
P.O. Box 115
Saanichton, B.C., Canada V8M 2C3
(800) 767-8658
www.scatmat.com

CSU/Denver County Cooperative Extension Master Gardener
110 16th Street #300
Denver, CO 80202
(720) 913-5278
www.colostate.edu/Depts/CoopExt/4DMG

Defenders of Wildlife, National Headquarters
1101 14th Street, NW #1400
Washington, D.C. 20005
(202) 682-9400
www.defenders.org

Delaware Division of Fish & Wildlife
89 Kings Highway
Dover, DE 19901
(302) 739-5072
www.dnrec.state.de.us

District of Columbia Fisheries and Wildlife Division
51 N Street, NE, 5th Floor
Washington, D.C. 20002-3323
(202) 535-2260
www.dchealth.com/dcfishandwildlife/welcome.htm

El Paso County Parks
2002 Creek Crossing
Colorado Springs, CO 80906
(719) 520-6375
www.co.el-paso.co.us/parks/reserve/reserve.asp

Farnam Co, Inc.
"Chaperone"
301 West Osborn Road
Phoenix, AZ 85013
(800) 234-2269
www.farnam.com

Florida Fish and Wildlife Commission
620 S. Meridian Street
Tallahassee, FL 32399-1600
(850) 488-2975
www.floridaconservation.org

Gallagher Power Fence, Inc.
P.O. Box 708900
San Antonio, TX 78270
(800) 531-5908
(210) 494-5211
www.gallagherusa.com

Georgia Department of Natural Resources
2070 U.S. Highway 278, SE
Social Circle, GA 30025
(770) 918-6401
www.dnr.state.ga.us

Greenway and Nature Center of Pueblo
5200 Nature Center Road
Pueblo, CO 81003
(719) 549-2443
www.pcc.cccoes.edu/ser_net/agencies/natcntr.htm

Hawaii Department of Land and Natural Resources
Kalanimoku Bldg.
1151 Punchbowl St.
Honolulu, HI 96813
(808) 587-0400
www.state.hi.us/dlnr/

Idaho Fish and Game Department
Box 25, 600 South Walnut
Boise, ID 83707
(208) 334-3700
www2.state.id.us/fishgame/fishgame.html

Illinois Department of Natural Resources
One Natural Resources Way
Springfield, IL 62702-1271
(217) 782-6232
www.dnr.state.il.us

Indiana Department of Natural Resources
402 West Washington Street, Rm W-273
Indianapolis, IN 46204
(317) 232-4020
www.state.in.us/dnr

International Wildlife Rehabilitation Council
4437 Central Place, Suite B-4
Suisun City, CA 94585-1633
(707) 864-1761
www.iwrc-online.org

Hunt Fencing Company
4635 Broadway
Eureka, CA 95503
(800) 200-3808
www.huntfencing.com

Intagra, Inc.
"Deer Away"
8500 Pillsbury Ave. South
Marty Proops
Bloomington, MN 55470
(800) 468-2472

International Association of Fish and Wildlife Agencies
444 North Capitol Street, NW, Suite 544
Washington, D.C. 20001
(202) 624-7890
www.iafwa.org/pagez.htm

Iowa Department of Natural Resources
Wallace State Office Building,
502 East 9th Street
Des Moines, IA 50319-0034
(515) 281-5918
www.state.ia.us/government/dnr/index.htm

Kansas Department of Wildlife and Parks
900 SW Jackson, Suite 502
Topeka, KS 66612-1233
(785) 296-2281
www.kdwp.state.ks.us

Kentucky Department of Fish and Wildlife Resources
One Game Farm Road
Frankfort, KY 40601
(502) 564-3400
(800) 858-1549
www.kdfwr.state.ky.us

Kildeer Police Department
22049 Chestnut Ridge
Kildeer, IL 60047
(847) 438-6644
www.kildeerpolice.com/kritters.htm

The Lady Bird Johnson Wildflower Center
4801 LaCrosse Avenue
Austin, TX 78739-1702
(512) 292-4200
www.wildflower.org

Louisiana Department of Wildlife and Fisheries
2000 Quail Drive
Baton Rouge, LA 70808
(225) 765-2925
www.wlf.state.la.us

Maine Department of Inland Fish and Wildlife
284 State Street, 41 State House Station
Augusta, ME 04333-0041
(207) 287-8000
www.state.me.us/ifw/index.html

Martin Ranch Supply
5980 Redwood Drive
Rohnert Park, CA 94928
(707) 585-1313
www.martinranchsupply.com

Maryland Department of Natural Resources
Tawes State Office Building
580 Taylor Avenue
Annapolis, MD 21401
(410) 260-8100
(877) 620-8367
www.dnr.state.md.us

Massachusetts Department of Fisheries
Wildlife and Environmental Law Enforcement
251 Causeway Street, Suite 400
Boston, MA 02114-2104
(617) 626-1590
www.state.ma.us/dfwele

Michigan Department of Natural Resources
P.O. Box 30028
Lansing, MI 48909-7944
(517) 373-1214
www.michigan.gov/dnr

Miller Chemical & Fertilizer Corp.
"Hot Sauce Animal Repellent"
P.O. Box 333
Hanover, PA 17331
(717) 632-8921
www.millerchemical.com

Minnesota Department of Natural Resources
Information Center
500 Lafayette Road
St. Paul, MN 55155-4040
(651) 296-6157
(888) MINNDNR
www.dnr.state.mn.us

Mission Wolf
P.O. Box 211
Silver Cliff, CO 82149
(719) 746-2919
www.firstax.com/mw/

Mississippi Department of Wildlife, Fisheries and Parks
1505 Eastover Drive
Jackson, MS 39211-6374
(601) 432-2400
www.mdwfp.com

Missouri Department of Conservation
P.O. Box 180
Jefferson City, MO 65102-0180
(573) 751-4115
www.conservation.state.mo.us

Montana Department of Fish, Wildlife and Parks
P.O. Box 200701
Helena, MT 59620-0701
(406) 444-3186
www.fwp.state.mt.us

Mountain Lion Foundation
P.O. Box 1896
Sacramento, CA 95812
(916) 442-2666
www.mountainlion.org

National Scent
"National Deer Repellant"
P.O. Box 667
San Jacinto, CA 92581-0667
(800) 338-8993
(909) 654-2442
www.nationalscent.com

National Wildlife Rehabilitators Association
14 North 7th Avenue
St. Cloud, MN 56303-4766
(320) 259-4086
www.nwrawildlife.org

Nebraska Game and Parks Commission
2200 North 33rd, Box 30370
Lincoln, NE 68503
(402) 471-0641
www.ngpc.state.ne.us

Nevada Department of Conservation and Natural Resources
123 West Nye Lane, Room 230
Carson City, NV 89706-0818
(775) 687-4360
www.state.nv.us/cnr

Nevada Division of Wildlife
Reno Headquarters
1100 Valley Road
Reno, NV 89512
(775) 688-1500
www.nevadadivisionofwildlife.org

New Hampshire Fish and Game Department
2 Hazen Drive
Concord, NH 03301
(603) 271-3211
www.wildlife.state.nh.us

New Jersey Division of Fish, Game and Wildlife
501 East State Street, 3rd Floor
Trenton, NJ 08625-0400
(609) 292-2965
(800) 927-6337
www.state.nj.us/dep/fgw

New Mexico Game and Fish Department
1 Wildlife Way
Sante Fe, NM 87507
(505) 476-8000
(800) 862-9310
www.gmfsh.state.nm.us

New York Department of Environmental Conservation
625 Broadway
Albany, NY 12233-1010
(518) 402-8924
www.dec.state.ny.us

New Zealand Fence Systems
23255 S.E. Highway 212
Boring, OR 97009
(800) 222-6849

North Carolina Department of Environment and Natural Resources
1601 Mail Service Center
Raleigh, NC 27699-1601
(919) 733-4984
www.enr.state.nc.us/

North Dakota Game and Fish Department
100 North Bismarck Expressway
Bismarck, ND 58501-5095
(701) 328-6300
www.state.nd.us/gnf/

Ohio Division of Wildlife
Fountain Square
Columbus, OH 43224
(614) 265-6565
www.dnr.state.oh.us/odnr

Oklahoma Department of Wildlife Conservation
1801 North Lincoln
Oklahoma City, OK 73105
(405) 521-2739
www.wildlifedepartment.com

Oregon Department of Fish and Wildlife
2501 SW First Avenue
Portland, OR 97207
(503) 872-5268
www.dfw.state.or.us

PAWS
P.O. Box 1037
Lynnwood, WA 98046
(425) 787-2500
www.paws.org/

Pennsylvania Fish and Boat Commission
1601 Elmerton Avenue
Harrisburg, PA 17110-9299
(717) 705-7800
www.state.pa.us/PA_Exec/Fish_Boat/pfbchom2.html

Performing Animal Welfare Society
P.O. Box 849
Galt, CA 95632
(202) 745-2606
www.pawsweb.org

PIGS: A Sanctuary
P.O. Box 629
Charlestown, WV 25414
(304) 262-0080
www.PIGS.org

Raptor Center of Pueblo
5200 Nature Center Road
Pueblo, CO 81003
(719) 549-2327

Rhode Island Department of Environmental Management
235 Promenade Street
Providence, RI 02908-5767
(401) 222-6800
(401) 222-3070
www.state.ri.us/dem/

South Carolina Department of Natural Resources
Rembert C. Dennis Building
1000 Assembly Street
Columbia, SC 29201
(803) 734-8888
www.dnr.state.sc.us/

South Dakota Game, Fish and Parks Department
523 East Capitol
Pierre, SD 57501-3182
(605) 773-3381
www.state.sd.us/gfp

SPCA of Texas
263 South Industrial Boulevard
Dallas, TX 75207
(214) 651-9611
www.spca.org

Suisun Marsh Wildlife Center
1171 Kellogg Street
Suisun, CA 94585
(707) 429-4295
www.suisunwildlife.org

Tennessee Wildlife Resources Agency
P.O. Box 40747
Nashville, TN 37204
(615) 781-6552
www.state.tn.us/twra

Texas Parks and Wildlife Department
4200 Smith School Road
Austin, TX 78744
(512) 389-4800
(800) 792-1112
www.tpwd.state.tx.us

The Gable's Raccoon World
www.geocities.com/RainForest/Vines/4892/

University of Florida
Cooperative Extension Service
Institute of Food and Agricultural Services
1038 McCarty Hall, P.O. Box 110210
Gainesville, FL 32611
(904) 392-1761
http://edis.ifas.ufl.edu

U.S. Fish and Wildlife Service
Office of Law Enforcement
4401 North Fairfax Drive, Room 500
Arlington, VA 22203
(703) 358-1949
www.le.fws.gov

U.S. Fish and Wildlife Services
http://offices.fws.gov

U-Spray, Inc.
4653 Highway 78
Lilburn, Georgia 30047
(770) 985-9388
www.bugspray.com

Utah Division of Wildlife Resources
1594 West North Temple
Salt Lake City, UT 84114-6301
(801) 538-4700
www.wildlife.utah.gov

Vermont Department of Fish and Wildlife
103 South Main Street, 10 South
Waterbury, VT 05671-0501
(802) 241-3700
www.anr.state.vt.us/fw/fwhome

Virgin Islands Coastal Management Program
45 Mars Hill, Rainbow Building
Fredriksted, St. Croix
U.S. Virgin Islands 00840
(340) 773-3450
www.viczmp.com

Virginia Department of Game and Inland Fisheries
4010 West Broad Street
Richmond, VA 23230
(804) 367-1000
www.dgif.state.va.us

Washington Department of Fish and Wildlife
600 Capitol Way North
Olympia, WA 98501-1091
(360) 902-2200
www.wa.gov/wdfw

West Virginia Division of Natural Resources
State Capitol Complex Building
1900 Kanawha Boulevard
Charleston, WV 25305-0060
(304) 558-3380
www.dnr.state.wv.us

Wild Bird Store
Mall of America
816 West 98th Street
Bloomington, MN 55420
www.thewildbirdstore.com
(866) 247-3768 (main phone number)

Wild Forever Foundation
8030 Industry Road
Colorado Springs, CO 80915
(719) 495-4477
www.wildforever.org

Wildcare, Inc.
P.O. Box 901
Lawrence, KS 66044
(913) 583-9800
www.wildcarekansas.org

Wildlife Rescue
RR #1, Perth Road
Ontario, Canada, K0H 2L0

Wildlife Rescue and Rehabilitation, Inc.
P.O. Box 1157
Boerne, TX 78006
(210) 698-1709
www.wildlife-rescue.org

Wildside Rehabilitation and Education Center
8601 Houston Road
Eaton Rapids, MI 48827
(517) 663-6153

Wisconsin Department of Natural Resources
101 South Webster Street
Madison, WI 53703
(608) 266-2621
www.dnr.state.wi.us

Wyoming Game and Fish Department
5400 Bishop Boulevard
Cheyenne, WY 82006
(307) 777-4600
http://gf.state.wy.us/

Xeriscape Garden Club
P.O. Box 5502
Austin, TX 78763
(512) 370-9505
www.zilker-garden.org/xgc/xgcinfo.html

Index